"I love this book and its author, Corey Blake, as he has a deep empathy for both the author and the reader with a goal of creating a peak experience for both. I've thought of Corey as a sherpa, the Himalayan guide that helps people trek to the peak, but with this book, I now see Corey as a trailblazer himself. You will be profoundly changed by reading this work of art."
—Chip Conley, Founder of Joie de Vivre Hospitality and *New York Times* Bestselling Author of *Emotional Equations*

"I have seldom seen someone so willing to expose themselves authentically—ESPECIALLY in a business niche book. I felt like I was reading a version of my own personal journey through the speaking of a kindred spirit. Corey's story is close enough for jazz."
—John King, CEO, Cultural Architecture and *New York Times* Bestselling Author of *Tribal Leadership*

"In my life I've always felt that I failed forward into better situations. Until I read *#Jump* I always thought I was just lucky. Corey will take you on a journey that shows what a humbling teacher pain and failure can be. This is a no-holds barred look into Corey's mirror. A mirror in which many of us will see ourselves. My guess is once you read *#Jump* you will end up on a more fulfilling path that leads you closer to your vision of success every single day."
—Carl Smith, Chief Keeper Upper, The nGen Works Company

"In *#Jump*, Corey shares his personal story of how he found his way to success. If you're an entrepreneur, a business owner, an artist, or an author, you can learn from Corey's story of creativity and innovation."
—Tony Hsieh, *New York Times* Bestselling Author of *Delivering Happiness*, CEO of Zappos.com, Inc.

"Through a highly gifted creative lens, Corey Michael Blake blasts away the doubts and fears most of us have about being true to ourselves. *#Jump* is a compelling story of risk and reward, of what it means to not accept defeat, to create even when we don't believe we can. Corey's willingness to open the door to his life and let us walk around, bump into things, and learn how to reach our true potential is a true gift."

—Rich Horwath, CEO, Strategic Thinking Institute, Author of
Deep Dive and *Strategy for You*

"Whenever I am truly impressed with a book I say to myself 'I wish I had written that!' and that is exactly what I said after I finished Corey Michael Blake's book *#Jump*. Corey's honesty and integrity in telling his story of struggle and achievement is an inspiration to anyone who has a story worth telling—which, as Corey observes, is truly everyone. As I contemplate working with Corey and his fabulous Round Table Team on my second book, I can only hope I have Corey's courage and the resolve necessary to tell my story. And I'm sure that with Corey's aid I will be able to do just that."

—Paul Glover, Founder of Glover & Associates, Author of
WorkQuake: Making the Seismic Shift to a "Knowledge Economy"

"We live in an incredible time where industries, career paths and life pursuits are being redefined, and Corey is blazing his own trails on how it can be done. If you ever questioned whether you can actually pursue your passion and make a lifelong journey, career and calling out of it, *#Jump* could be the inspiration for that leap of faith to finally get you started."

—Jenn Lim, CEO and Chief Happiness Officer, Delivering Happiness

"Corey Blake is a master storyteller. If you like stories (and who doesn't?) you'll be captivated by *#Jump*. Intertwined are the life lessons he has learned as well as ones we can learn from. This is a book you'll want to share, just make sure you get it back."
—Bobette Gorden, Vice President, Influence at Work

"Corey's engaging voice and raw honesty engages us in his struggle to embrace a creative life, and inspires us when he makes his leap. This is a worthwhile read for anyone who has ever been tempted to scratch that creative itch."
—Patrick Ross, Award-Winning Journalist, Blogger, and Creative Writer on Creativity

"Corey invites us to celebrate the many lessons learned in life, creativity, and business through his journey 'jumping' in pursuit of building a world-class company that affects lives on a grand scale. He not only demonstrates that we don't need someone else's permission to change the world, but explores the evolution of Round Table Companies' transformation process—blending storytelling, art, truth, and play—which illuminate the epiphanies that express our individual uniqueness and the stories that make us visible to one another, connect us, and empower us to be human together. Hope you heed Corey's wisdom and *Jump* into your life."
—Si Alhir, Author, Enterprise Transformation Coach & Consultant, Creating WE Institute (CWI) Associate & Member, and CultureSync Approved Tribal Leader

"If anyone thinks there is a common path to becoming an entrepreneur, they obviously don't know Corey Blake. A classic failure to triumph story, with a fun modern twist."
—Seth Kravitz, Founder, Technori

"It's not every day that you read a book that encourages you to jump. But that is Corey Michael Blake's ambitious plea at the start of *Jump: Creativity lessons from 9000 feet*. By sharing his own exhilarating personal stories of jumping—and sometimes falling—Corey paves the way for you to make your own jump into the unknown."

—Melanie Sklarz, Founder of DoseofCreativity.com

"*#Jump* leaves me gasping for air! With the precision and vision of a mountain climber to reach heights, Corey's journey and results are breathtaking. When he returns safely, I feel his triumph and this invites me to take the leap and delve into my own creativity, purpose, and voice."

—Lynne Feingold, Founder, SingYoJoy; Executive Coach and Manager, Coaching Services, Department of Treasury's Executive Institute

"Creativity is a risky business. It is fueled by failure. Its fire is stoked by a belief in the unseen and unproven. In spite of these risks, a few daring souls choose to innovate and push the rest of us to experience the world differently. Corey Michael Blake is one of those people and in his memoir, *#Jump* he takes you through his 'hang-on-to-your-hat' journey from struggling actor to CEO and Founder of Round Table Companies. With a refreshing humility and transparency, Blake's insight into how to embrace our passions and transform great ideas into sound business both inspires and challenges. This is more than a business story, however. It is a story about how to embrace the possibilities of creativity that exist within all of us to transform how we work and how we live."

—Dr. Doug Bolton, Principal, North Shore Academy

#JUMP
Creativity lessons from 9000 feet

Corey Michael Blake

with Annie Hart & Katie Gutierrez Painter

#JUMP: CREATIVITY LESSONS FROM 9000 FEET

Copyright © 2012 Corey Michael Blake
Writers of the Round Table Press

Published by:

Writers of the Round Table Press Inc.   www.RoundTableCompanies.com
1670 Valencia Way   www.CoreyMichaelBlake.com
Mundelein, IL 60060   Phone: 815.346.2398

*Writers of the Round Table Press and logo are trademarks of Round Table Companies
and Writers of the Round Table Inc.*

Cover design by Analee Paz
Interior design and layout, back cover by Sunny DiMartino

Printed in the United States of America

ISBN Paperback: 978-1-61066-050-1

No part of this publication may be reproduced or transmitted in any form or by any means,
mechanical or electronic, including photocopying and recording, or by any information
storage and retrieval system, without permission in writing from author or publisher
(except by a reviewer, who may quote brief passages and/or show brief video clips in a review).

For those who have jumped into
the unknown by my side.

TABLE OF CONTENTS

INTRODUCTION — vii
AUTHOR'S NOTE — xiii

PART I: HOLLYWOOD

#JUMP 1	Elevation 9000	1
#JUMP 2	Good Intentions	15
#JUMP 3	A Stubborn Cliché	19
#JUMP 4	Naïveté	27
#JUMP 5	Inner Pain Reaching Out	31
#JUMP 6	Mismatched Values	37

PART II: A CHANGE IN SCENERY

#JUMP 7	Too Much a Businessman	45
#JUMP 8	Professional Boundaries	51
#JUMP 9	Trailblazing	55
#JUMP 10	Being the Devil in My Own Deal	63
#JUMP 11	Getting the Sale vs. Doing the Work	73
#JUMP 12	*From the Barrio to the Board Room and the Transformational Power of Story*	83

AFTERWORD — 93
ABOUT THE AUTHOR — 97

INTRODUCTION

AT the time I started working on this book, I was the thirty-five-year-old president and founder of a four-year-old company that I was desperately trying to hold together. I had a client who owed me a small fortune, a couple dozen subcontractors I was trying to keep working in a recession, and a core staff being pushed to learn new skills in an effort to keep the company afloat. Meanwhile, we were trying to figure out who we were, educating our clients—and ourselves—about how we could change their lives. Now, as I near the book's completion, I am nearly thirty-eight and riding a tidal wave of excitement around our unique book writing, graphic novel, and publishing models.

2011 found Round Table Companies covered in *The New York Times, Wall Street Journal, USA Today, Inc., Forbes, Publishers Weekly, Chicago Sun-Times, Barron's* and on Fox News and Bloomberg TV. We've redefined how book writing can be accomplished, how businesses can communicate, and how storytelling bridges the great divide between us as humans. Our great exposure came as the result of a huge swing we took when we started licensing best-selling non-fiction books and converting them into the graphic novel/comic book format. But our core business is in helping thought leaders write their books using a model that big publishers and individual writers cannot compete with.

At Round Table, we've created a methodology that utilizes a filmmaker's collaborative approach, which relieves clients from the traditional avenues of holing up in a cabin for six months or hiring a ghostwriter and then trying to manage the project while just hoping for the best. We've taken the fear and overwhelm out of writing by constructing an environment conducive to success. We surround a would-be author—traditionally a non-fiction thought leader—with a team of experts who guide the process. The end result is countless epiphanies and a transformational process that culminates in a dynamic and intimate experience for readers that connects them deeply with the author.

I'm going to paraphrase Harold Clurman, founder of the Group Theatre in NY back in 1931 whose movement eventually led to Broadway and movies as we now know them. Harold said that the truth is like castor oil: it's bitter and hard to swallow. And so we open their mouths with entertainment, and while they're open, we pour it in.

Harold Clurman, as a generator of storytelling, has been profoundly influential in my life. He crystallized my understanding of the value of art. Of our ability to use the craft of storytelling to inform, educate, and inspire people in a venue where they expected to simply be entertained. With that realization has come a great responsibility that I feel to the stories of the world. As Michael Margolis, founder of GetStoried.com and the Dean of Story University puts it, "We're all on our own hero's journey." And I'll add to that by saying when we share our stories we become visible to one another. When we share the "why," the "how," and the "with whom" behind our passion, behind our choice of livelihood, behind the causes we fight for, we claim our voice in a way that demands a positive or negative emotional response from those around us. Storytelling adds dimension to us in a world that often seems not to care if we're invisible.

My introduction to storytelling started back at Millikin University, where I graduated with a BFA in Theatre. Millikin was an amazing stomping ground for me, and I credit Denise Myers with teaching me to understand the art of play; Barry Pearson, whose Shakespeare classes taught me the rhythm of words; and Laura Ledford, who led me to find my voice as an actor. Without them, I couldn't help authors become comfortable exploring their ideas and inevitably finding their voices in their writing.

It was in my senior year at Millikin that I starred in the play *Jeffrey* (sometimes affectionately referred to as "The Gay Play"). As the leading role, I was on stage for the entire play, a solid two hours, and I had to make out with my freshman year roommate, Matt. I remember his scratchy face. I was straight, and so was Matt, but our director, Scott, was one of the few men in the theatre department who was openly gay at that time and he loved milking that make-out scene.

Two months after our version of the play closed, I was in my college apartment when I received a call from a neighboring playhouse about ninety minutes away. They were putting on a production of *Jeffrey*, and their lead had fallen ill. They had a sold-out house of three hundred that night and wanted to know if I would lead their production so they wouldn't be forced to cancel their show. I don't know where the courage came from, since two months had gone by and I couldn't possibly remember all the lines, but I'm thankful to this day that I said yes. That my director Scott drove me and ran lines with me in the car on the way. That we were able to block the show that afternoon and that I rocked the house that night. I was fearless. And that experience taught me about showing up in Art, and striving for brilliance with no excuses.

After my education at Millikin, I headed off to Hollywood, where I would stay for ten years, being shaped both by the storytelling world of the thirty-second commercials I acted in as well as the film and television world, where I dabbled and learned about the highest standards in storytelling and about the crafting of moments in time. My continued training at Playhouse West, under the tutelage of Christopher Liebe and Jeff Goldblum, taught me profound lessons about truth in art and the current beneath the words; the one we cannot explain, but can deeply feel when an artist finds it and rides it.

Storytelling, Art, Truth, Play. These are the cornerstones of the creative. And as creatives, we focus on them with nearly all our time and effort as we navigate our education in Art. Then we're released into the big world with no understanding of business. And like a series of slaps in the face, we're forced to either give up (as too many do) or to arrive at new lessons and use them to thrive.

All of these lessons in acting, filmmaking, and eventually in book writing informed my building of Round Table Companies so that we could take our creative minds and direct them at real-world problems. Our VP, David Cohen, his wife, Erin, who is our Director of Happiness, and I are all theatre majors who have turned to business for our own self-actualization. And our executive editor, Katie Gutierrez Painter, has an MFA in fiction. All four of us had a rich history steeped in creativity before we transferred to business. You see, acting and writing are often all about the individual. But art, for my team and for me, is far more impacting when we use our storytelling expertise to help others to express their lives' missions and the brilliant work they are engaged in. We create experiences for people, and we're charged with packaging our authors' genius in a way that lets audiences quickly see and feel who they are at their core.

I've always been amazed at how many gatekeepers there are who prevent people from sharing their stories. In Hollywood, there were agents and casting directors and studio execs. In publishing, there are agents and editors and publishers, and until now the system was built to keep most people out. When I broke through in acting and was invited to the inner world, I found that it wasn't particularly special. That I had fought for what ended up being an illusion. And that fight took years from my life as I headed in that misguided direction. My goal in forming Round Table has always been to help save people from the illusion that they need someone else's permission to change the world. Sometimes they just need accountability and the expertise of a loving and nurturing team of professionals who believe in the value of their story. Today, when the stock market is a volatile disaster, people are more willing to invest in themselves and their stories, their personal brands and their lives. To them I say *bravo! Cheers! L'chaim!*

In his bestselling book, *Peak: How Great Companies Get Their Mojo from Maslow*, hotelier Chip Conley describes our ability to create peak experiences for our customers and employees and that those peak experiences create "lifelong inspiration, evangelism, and pride of ownership." At Round Table, we have designed an environment that encourages those peak experiences to arise in moments of storytelling epiphany, moments that can be grabbed and harnessed to inform the final experience our authors are creating for their specific audience. Since the inception of our organization, I have stressed that if an author doesn't profoundly change through the writing of their book, we cannot expect a reader to change through reading it.

I invite you to journey with me through the lessons that allowed me to create this new storytelling business model. Lessons in creativity, in business, in life. I've made some big hairy audacious mistakes, some stupid mistakes, and, at least partially because of them, my first two companies fell apart and none of the movies I produced or directed made it to the audience they deserved. I've spent months in bed feeling overly dramatic. I've abused drugs to escape my reality and avoid growing up. I've emotionally vomited on everyone around me. Hell, I spent two years trying to force the world to bend to me. It didn't. Instead, I was forced to admit that talent and good intentions were not enough, and that admission allowed me to change direction and survive.

I am defined not by my successes. Nor by my failures. It is my continual willingness to jump that defines me. Through these pages, you'll journey with me as I jump so high only to find my body flattened and crushed by the earth upon impact. This book is a celebration of the lessons learned as I found the strength to jump again in my pursuit of the knowledge and wisdom necessary to build a world-class company and affect lives on a grand scale.

I hope that in reading these pages, you'll find your own inner hero—and your jackass, your critic, your drama queen, your champion, your liar, and your dreamer. Mostly, I hope that my stories, that these pages, light a fire beneath you to find your own voice and jump with me. Jump into that new business. Jump into your story. Jump into your voice. Jump into your life.

Corey Michael Blake
corey@roundtablecompanies.com
October 30, 2011

AUTHOR'S NOTE

THIS book was created using a process I developed over the course of a decade spent working in film and publishing. Traditionally, our company acts as a story guide for our clients, surrounding them with as many as ten different experts throughout the writing process so it is joyous, easy, and full of epiphany. To tell my own story, I had to enter the role of the client—and so I hired Annie Hart to be my story guide and our Executive Editor, Katie Gutierrez Painter, worked with my words. We spent seven months on weekly telephone calls, during which Annie helped extract the depth of my story and lessons as Katie listened, and then another five months where Katie and I worked together to shape my stories into what you're about to read. This book is entirely in my voice, true to my experiences; however, because of these two dynamic women and a host of other caring professionals, it is exponentially greater than anything I could have delivered on my own. I hope you feel all of us in this book.

PART I

HOLLYWOOD

#J^UMP 1

ELEVATION 9000

OUTSIDE the cabin, skiers in bright puffy suits zipped across the mountains, their cheeks reddened by the snow and winter air at 7,900 feet. But the nine of us holed up inside the cabin weren't there to ski. We were there to do something even more invigorating, even more joyful—we were there to create.

It was 2001, and I had been living in L.A. since 1996 and working regularly as an actor since 1999. By the time I joined the others in that cabin, I had shot between eight and ten national commercials, many of which had paid tens of thousands of dollars. It felt like easy money: I'd go to a set, shake some hands, get set up, rehearse for ten or fifteen minutes, go back to the trailer while the crew lit the scene, act for twenty or thirty minutes, and then go home. I was the only one of my close friends who didn't have a day job much of the time. Acting was paying my bills, just as I'd dreamed about in college. I was working a few days a year, auditioning twice a day, and making a full-time salary. Most people

1

would kill to be in that position. And yet I felt lost, satiated in the short term but confused in the long term. That kind of acting wasn't what I'd gone to L.A. to do. I didn't want to be a commercial superstar-there was no journey in it.

The recognition of my unhappiness often hit hardest when I was sitting in my trailer. For the two, three, four, five, six, seven hours I'd wait to act for those precious few minutes, I'd be thinking, *Okay, well, this stinks. What time is it? I need to sit here. Let me keep myself busy. Let me run my lines. Okay, I'm working my lines. Maybe I'll open the trailer door, maybe there's someone I know! Okay, there's not. I'll close the door. Let me take a piss. Okay, another hour's gone by; maybe they'll call me soon. Let me turn on the TV. Oh, there's crappy reception and nothing worth watching. Guess I'll just lie down on the little cot. I can't sleep. I'll go outside and take a walk and say hi to a couple of people. I'll stand on the set and watch. Put my hands in my pockets. Watch watch watch.*

What I saw as I stood on set was that everyone but me had a job to do. I didn't exist. I was invisible.

Well, now another hour's gone by. Let me go back to my trailer. Oh, God, this is torture. My phone's ringing! "Oh, hey, what's up? Yeah, this is so cool. I know. Livin' the life!" I'd hang up the phone and try to pretend it was cool but it wasn't cool at all; it was terrible. My whole body was rebelling. *This feels bad*, my body was telling me. *It feels wrong; it's just not me.* I was drawn to tears on that little cot in my trailer, thinking, *This is it? This is what I'm fighting for?* After a life of training and working toward this dream, the realization that I was a nobody, that I was irrelevant, was brutal.

Acting was never supposed to feel like a job. It was supposed to be magical and fun, and my opinion was supposed to be important and sought after. But during those low points in the trailer, I recognized that it was only a paycheck. Hollywood was a permission-based business where I was always trying to get the job, and then once I did, it was fun and glamorous for about ten minutes, but mostly, it was a job.

When I played leading roles in independent films, the hours in my trailer were a reprieve. Time for me to make a phone call or just breathe. And I knew everyone on set, so I could easily hang out with others who had downtime. But for commercials and smaller parts on TV shows, I was on a set for a day or two, three at most. I didn't know anyone. I had no pre-existing relationships. I wasn't part of the family; I was a short-term guest whom no one was ever sorry to see leave.

At the time, a part of me thought I should just shut up and suffer through my disillusionment, that it was a good thing I had going. I had been so broke for so long, piecing together money from odd jobs—restaurant job here, handyman's assistant job there—and ultimately living on maybe $12,000 a year. But as I worked on those national commercials, trips to the mailbox were *fun*. I'd get checks for thousands of dollars at a time, and sometimes they'd come every day. I remember having a $36,000 year when I did my first couple of acting jobs. In retrospect, I see that's a starting salary for most people at a regular job, but at the time I thought, *Ooh, I'm making all this money having fun!* But the only actual fun part about it was dreaming that it was all going to lead somewhere amazing.

In the meantime, though, I had to face that I was a nobody on set, that I was completely replaceable and totally irrelevant most of the time. Fear gripped me. What if everybody else, my friends and family, found that out? What if they realized that my so-called success was all a ruse? So

#JUMP

I acted all the time, with everyone I knew, just trying to keep up the façade. It made so much sense to me back then. I needed everyone around me to believe that *It* was happening for me. I needed to feel on top. Playing into the illusion became easier than admitting the reality: that I was miserable and terrified that this was where the dream would end.

Thankfully, in those days, I found relief from those trailer-hours in an acting class I was taking at Playhouse West. Class was three hours, twice a week, but we students needed to put in fifteen to twenty hours a week minimum to improve our craft; the class was a time for us to make adjustments. So, because I was a working actor and didn't have a day job much of the time, I hosted a lot of rehearsals at my place.

My apartment was a dynamite two-bedroom on the coolest street in Hollywood—Beachwood Avenue, right under the Hollywood sign. The apartment had been passed along from friend to friend to friend, and by the time I moved in, the place was already steeped in history among those of us who had moved to L.A. after college. The entire place had thin, old, dirty blue carpet. Most of the time, I walked around barefoot, and my feet were often black with grime. I didn't care. Much more important to me was the feeling of living in the hills, the balcony with a great view of surrounding apartment buildings, and the characters on my street smoking cigarettes on breezy California nights.

Nearly seven days a week, my acting classmates showed up. We'd all chat for a few minutes, and then people would split off in pairs to different rooms: two people in my bedroom, two in the second bedroom, two in the living room, and two in the kitchen. Paired off this way, we did exercises called "doors and activities." In them, one person is doing something personal and important when another person, who is also extremely intent, interrupts that activity with a need they are not allowed to directly express.

Here's a good example activity. I have to leave for court in thirty-five minutes. I'm suing an insurance company that is refusing to pay for an accident that nearly crippled me and temporarily prevented me from working. My attorney has just called and told me that the insurance company found a witness who is going to testify that she saw me skiing after the accident. So now I have an hour to go through nearly seven hundred pages of documentation and piece together a timeline that proves she saw me *before* the accident, not after. I'm in the middle of this highly emotional, important task when there's a knock on the door. It's the second actor, who desperately needs something from me. But I can't tell the other person what I'm working on, and that person can't tell me what he needs. All we can do is identify how we're feeling and respond to how the other person is behaving.

This experience can be incredibly intense because you've got two people on desperate missions who can't deflate the scene through explanation. It was natural, super-heightened conflict. In essence, these exercises aimed to find truth in the moment rather than take the three-second pause that we do in life to question our instincts before responding to a person or situation politely.

In college, I had been taught to break down a script, learn the lines, and act out what I thought the emotional journey was. But this new approach was teaching me how to live in the moment and not react to *what* someone was saying but rather *how* that person was saying it. I was forced to discern how the other person was emotionally coming at me, which is the true journey beneath the dialogue of a script.

#J^UMP

When my circumstances in these exercises were strong enough, the emotional ride was so unexpected and intense that it might last for days. I'd feel like a gaping wound, so raw and inflamed that if the breeze blew at me from the wrong direction, it could bring me to tears or belly-laughter or fury. I could feel an immense wave of attraction or revulsion toward somebody in the middle of an exercise. It's a crazy thing to say, but the amount of intense emotion sometimes made a couple start kissing or made another break down crying together. We just couldn't help ourselves. Living in this heightened state of reality was such beautiful stuff, yet it was incredibly terrifying to live so vulnerably in that space of openness. In many ways, I felt more alive then than during any other time in my life.

One day, after everyone from acting class left my apartment, another actor named Lisa stayed behind. We started talking more personally, as artists with bad boundaries often do, and we got on to the subject of dreams. I felt compelled to show her a video that I couldn't get off my mind.

Harold Clurman, a theatre director and drama critic, had created a family of actors, directors, and writers, including Elia Kazan, Clifford Odetts, Lee Strasberg, Stella Adler, and other titans of the New York theatre world. He was known as "the generator" and was the person who fueled the engine and inspired the machine—the people—to work. All of the different parts of the machine needed to be *inspired* to bring their best, and Clurman was a dynamic leader who directed them all to action.

The video about him, which I'd first seen in college, was twenty-eight minutes long, and I sat next to Lisa feeling mesmerized, as though I was seeing some kind of destiny for myself. For the first time, I was able to express what I was after: creating a family of artists. It was something I was already doing, to some extent, by organizing these rehearsals and inspiring people to do good work while they were there, but in that moment, I recognized that I needed to take it further.

When the video ended, I told Lisa, "I need to do something bigger."

I need to do something bigger. It was the first time I'd said those words out loud, and there was an inevitability to them. Soon, I was spearheading the conversation with a larger group of my classmates, and we agreed that we wanted to become educated together in storytelling so that we could pave our own paths in the movie world. I decided to use some of my commercial acting money to invite these actors with me on a storytelling, creative journey—the journey of finding out what that "something bigger" was. I remember standing at my kitchen table, writing down our plans on a yellow legal pad, and within a week, the event was scheduled: the nine of us would go to a cabin in Mammoth Mountain, California, for one week.

Let me introduce you to the cast of characters.

There was Fro, an Egyptian kid whose real name was Mark but who earned his nickname through a big ridiculous explosion of hair. Usually stoned, Fro was the most easily lovable member of our group, and he added a youthful innocence to the experience. Everyone adored him.

Brad was a big, heavy, goateed bear of a guy. He was constantly smoking and looked like a famous country music singer. His father was an executive with Anheuser-Busch, so Brad was an all-business kind of guy. He was confident, even cocky, and often a douche bag, but I loved him. He was my right-hand man—loyal, reliable, and funny as hell.

#JUMP

Chris was one of the acting teachers at our school. He was conservative and religious; a sweet guy with an eye for talent and a deep understanding of the acting technique we were being taught.

Christina was an ass-kicking Texan girl. She was smart, sexy, and full of sass. She was fun to work with, incredibly reliable, and bold in her beliefs.

Cambria was a part-time nurse, quiet and kind. She preferred being in the background most of the time but was a little tornado when she hit her sweet spot onstage.

John was the rugged "manly man" of the group. Older and wiser, with a successful salon business he ran with his wife, John was a strong actor and the head of our class.

Ward was passionate, bullheaded, arrogant, and a hard worker. I saw him as a younger version of myself. He was a devastatingly serious guy who, perhaps paradoxically, wanted to make people laugh more than anything else. Ward was a strong asset, though he infuriated me on numerous occasions.

Finally, there was Lisa. She was twelve years older than me, on the rocks with her husband, and I thought I loved her desperately. We fell hard for each other in acting class, and my passion to save her from a troubled marriage lulled me into thinking I was a hero. Our secret affair and the drama surrounding it fueled my passion as an artist. I thought I could do anything and felt empowered by my good intentions.

With the wind at my back, I led the group to Mammoth.

Together in the cabin, we were an electric (and eclectic!) combination of personalities—full of ideas and inspired to be part of what we were building. We created our own universe inside that cabin, an entire lifestyle that supported our purpose. I had prepared menus for each meal, we went shopping together, and we designated who was responsible for cooking throughout the week, followed by who would clean up. We built fires, shared stories, and learned together, with different people in charge of different lesson plans. Amid our learning was laughter and silliness, a growing bond that made the process of creating a joy. For those days, the nine of us were a family. We had to take care of each other both professionally and emotionally while also getting great work done.

Mornings, we rose early and gathered in the main living area with our hair still mussed from sleep. Coffee was passed around, and we'd start with a writing exercise or a video on storytelling. Then we'd go our separate ways and clean up for a bit before reuniting for breakfast and conversation. All of our talk was about creating, about sharing our stories. We'd continue that process of education, exploration, and sharing late into the night. After dinner, we usually played spoons, got drunk, and opened up a bit more of ourselves to the group.

On the third day there, I got a call from my commercial agent: I had booked a commercial job for Miller Light and needed to leave to film it. It was intended to be a major spot, with multiple commercials, which meant a big payday. I hated the idea of leaving but trusted that the opportunity was meant to be; so, on the fourth day, I left. The eight others stayed on for another couple of days, learning and brainstorming together. It was ironic—I had created the experience, and I was the first who had to leave it. I had created a family of dreamers and a new home, and here I was being pulled back into the world of commercial acting that I didn't want. Ah, the lure of money.

Once we were all back in L.A., however, the connection we'd forged at the cabin remained strong. Armed with three film ideas that we were all passionate about, we decided to formalize the structure of our group. We established a company called Elevation 9000 Films, an homage to the cabin in which many of us had felt a rebirth.

After that, our acting rehearsals became less frequent. Instead, my apartment turned into the site for meetings in which we transferred from a performance mindset to a production agenda. Now thinkers and visionaries from another side, we'd sit in my large living room (with Brad and Fro on the balcony smoking cigarettes), create together, and figure out the best ways to get our films made and out into the world.

Ward was the most passionate about the script he had been working on with Fro. He wanted to direct it and we agreed, as a group, to move forward with the project. I remember being up late at night and early in the morning sending script notes back and forth with Ward and Fro. It was my first time developing a piece of intellectual property, and I felt electric with the film's potential.

The film, called *The Boy Scout*, was about the battle between the evil of the world and the Boy Scout, who, despite his huge mission to save humanity from the Evil Yokono, couldn't turn away from the simpler good deeds of rescuing a young girl's cat from a tree or stopping a woman from burning her pork chops. Ward played the Boy Scout, I was the Eagle Scout, Fro played Cubby (the Cub Scout), and Christina played the Evil Yokono. Brad, Christina, and I were executive producers, and Ward was our director. Christina was a bulldozer—the single greatest force in getting the film made—both financially and logistically, for which she deserves tremendous credit. Cambria produced alongside Christina, and Lisa had a small role in the film and lent production support, as did Christopher and John.

I pushed my high standards on everyone, as did Ward and Christina, and the entire group met our desire to raise the bar. I was excited to put together a fun project that was also a legitimate film. We created a professional press kit in a glossy white folder with the Elevation 9000 Films logo embossed in gold on the front. It included a description of our project and team, and a phenomenal *Boy Scout* poster that featured a picture of the Boy Scout and Cubby, resplendent in their uniforms with a stark red background behind them. We used the kit to attract a professional Hollywood stunt team, one of Stephen Spielberg's assistant costume designers, and an award-winning cinematographer, among others. Attracting that level of talent to our project made me feel proud, impressive, and worthy.

For the next year, we all worked tirelessly to bring the film to the screen. There were forty-five people on set every day, including the nine of us. Many relationships were formed—some people were fighting, some were forging love affairs, and others were embroiled in hate affairs. Lisa and I were still hiding our own affair from everybody else; when Christina discovered our relationship during production, she faithfully carried the unfair burden for the sake of the film. Binding us all together was our belief in the project.

The Boy Scout turned out to be part action, part comedy, and a lot of heart. Fro found a composer who put together wonderful heartfelt music that juxtaposed brilliantly with the comedy and action. The result, I felt, was incredible. Each of us had a piece of ownership in that final product. Ward wanted to make people laugh, and I wanted to inspire them. The film felt like a fair balance of our personalities, mixed in with the wonderful attributes of everyone who had contributed to the project.

#J^UMP

We showed *The Boy Scout* at our acting school's annual film festival. To my knowledge, our group was the first from our school to put together a full ensemble, high quality, stylized product like this. After the credits rolled in front of three hundred of our peers, the eruption from the audience was one of the greatest feelings I've ever experienced. The film had been our home, the group our family, for the last year of our lives, and to have created something that worked the way *The Boy Scout* did cemented every belief I had about what the creative journey was supposed to be.

Then Ward decided to change the film's music to something more comedic, more slapstick. When I first heard the new music, my gut reaction was dramatic and full of expletives. I hated it. But more than the music itself, I hated that it was never put up for discussion to the group. The situation took me from feeling on top of the world to feeling churned up in its molten core. Ward was the director, but I—as the head of the company—had failed to create a contract that detailed who had the final decision on such matters because I believed that we could be most effective as a democracy. I was wrong. Without a clear delineation, we all had our own opinions about whose choice it was. And I was learning quickly that without clear structure, creative people fill the void with drama.

In the end, I felt that the movie went from inspiring hope to providing a useless chuckle, and I took Ward's dissention personally. His decision seemed to make the movie all about him instead of about us, as a family. I acted out accordingly, creating allies and preparing for battle. Meanwhile, others in the company were slowly finding out about my relationship with Lisa and were rightfully questioning my judgment. I had let them down by putting myself ahead of our film-family and deserved to lose their trust. So they were preparing for battle, too.

What I came to articulate later about the music for the film was that it symbolized who we were as filmmakers, as *storytellers,* and as people. And it turned out that all of us were different. We each had different core values, different passions, different strengths and weaknesses, and different agendas that were being expressed through our work. Until then, most of us had never been pushed to articulate any of that, and the filmmaking process brought it all to the surface to be dealt with. We were actors learning to be businesspeople, suddenly at each other's throats. Most of us, including me, made a bloody mess of it but somehow we all justified our actions every step of the way.

To look back at everything we accomplished, only to arrive at that point, was heartbreaking. It still is. The meaning of the film changed for me, as did the meaning of our once tight-knit group of creatives. With dramatic panache, the company that I loved quickly tore itself apart.

The film went on and played the festival circuit—it even won some prestigious awards—but no longer were nine people showing up to champion it. The family had been corrupted by my failure. The project was lost. The dream was lost. I had fallen flat, broken every bone and the dreamer in me wasn't sure he'd ever walk again.

#J^UMP 2

GOOD INTENTIONS

HERE are a few things you should understand about my childhood: I wasn't sexually abused; I wasn't abducted by aliens; my parents weren't alcoholics, and they're still married. But everybody has a trauma, and that trauma is a solid ten out of ten on a personal scale of pain.

On my fifth birthday, my mother came home with a cherry-covered cheesecake. After she, my father, my sister, and I had eaten dinner, she presented it to me. But I took one look at the cake and said, "I don't like cherries." Immediately, my mother sent me upstairs to my small room in our townhouse. A few minutes later, she stormed up, flung open my bedroom door, and started screaming at me. I don't remember her words, but she grabbed the door and slammed it, over and over again, as she yelled. I can still hear her voice rising as the door swung open and quieting as it closed. Gusts of air ruffled my bowl haircut as I cowered in the corner of the room. Many years later, when I asked my sister for her recollection of that day, she replied, "There was a lot of door slamming back then."

That was the year that my mother had a breakdown. She was depressed and moody and could fly into a rage when moments earlier she'd been fine. Eventually, she went through five weeks of hospitalization, but the lesson had already been taught to me: avoid, at all costs, upsetting those around you.

That lesson became even more crucial in the years after my mother's breakdown. In its aftermath, my parents set up a household where that kind of tumult could never occur again. We were taught that intention is what matters, not outcome—which meant, of course, that we could never be angry with anyone in our family; after all, the *intention* was always, undoubtedly, good.

All of this created some strong and lasting behaviors in me. When I moved to L.A. after college to pursue a career in acting, I presented myself as someone who could never offend. I was always the guy with good intentions—believing that was enough. But I was also a deliberate list-keeper. I'd make long mental lists of pros and cons. How many great things did I do throughout the pre-production of a film, for example? Far too many for anybody to fault me. That imbalance was my intentional way of avoiding accountability.

This technique worked reasonably well more than ninety-nine percent of the time. Inevitably, I became a workaholic as I pushed that positive agenda. I was convinced that no one could hold anything against a guy who was working fourteen to eighteen hour days for the good of the team. Even when I failed, it wasn't for lack of trying.

The danger was that my technique was so effective. People found it extremely difficult to get upset with me ... until the big stones toppled. Not having the right contracts in place for *The Boy Scout,* dating women involved in films I produced—the fallout of these mistakes was so great that my pro-list was chucked out the window as people inevitably blew up at me or at one another. In those moments, I was so shocked and unprepared. *But my list is so long!* I thought. *How could you get upset?* My intentions *were* good.

In a way, the last thirty years have been atonement for my failing to appreciate that cherry-covered cheesecake. I've spent my life—and certainly most of my career—focusing entirely on other people's dreams and needs. For a year, two years, three years, or more, I'm emotionally keyed into each of my clients, helping them tell their stories and then build their audience. It's extraordinarily fulfilling, but in the end, I'm not accountable if a reader doesn't *like* the story. I can nurture my client through the metaphorical slamming of that door, but I don't have to feel the excruciating pain myself.

Through the help of a patient wife, an excellent therapist, and the writing of this book, I've recently realized how pervasive these patterns of behavior have been in my life. It's time for me to grow up. It's time for me to metamorphose from boy to man. Most people think this kind of transition—and the thrilling, terrifying exploration and self-discovery that accompany it—is what you're "supposed to do" in your twenties. Yet many of us, including me, struggle with individual growth every day. That's tragic because our personal traumas can imprison us forever if we don't constantly work hard at changing our behavior.

Recently, I confronted my mother about that rocky time in our lives. "When you had your breakdown," I told her, "I learned to tiptoe around you."

"Yeah," she replied wryly, "so did your father."

#JUMP

How amazing, I thought, that my mother wasn't defensive. She could admit what had happened and how her actions had influenced our family. Healing began for me that day and over the last two years, I've been working to *see* the five-year-old boy rather than *be* the five-year-old boy. I can often be an adult in the room with my younger self and hold his hand while he feels terrified of other people's anger. Granted, I can't *always* manage it; in fact, I often make a mess of it, but I do enjoy trying and feel tremendous pride when I recognize what I'm doing in the moment.

Intentionally examining your past and using it to change behaviors and become a happier adult—well, that has nothing to do with art. Or maybe it has everything to do with art. After all, this book project is the first thing I've ever done that, at the core, starts with me. Talk about a leap of faith. I want freedom from my perceived childhood failure. I don't want to feel like a hostage to that scared little boy and what he thought the world was teaching him about good intentions. If the door gets slammed this time, it'll be on me … and that's a beautiful thing.

#J^UMP 3

A STUBBORN CLICHÉ

SIX months into my depression after Elevation 9000 Films collapsed, the dreamer in me emerged from a fog of self-pity. Working with Brad and Chris from my previous venture, we created the Elevation 9000 Film Lab. Twice a week, Playhouse West let us meet in a lab environment with other actors who wanted to build films. Thirty students paid monthly to be there, and we walked them through the process of developing their scripts. I felt useful again, fueled by students who needed guidance that I could offer.

After many months of creative development, there were two films that the students wanted to make. One of them had an $8,000 budget, and Chris accepted the opportunity to direct the film. The other project had $35,000 behind it, and I was asked to help make *Gretchen Brettschneider Skirts Thirty*, a film that explored one woman's fear of turning thirty.

#JUMP

Annie—the leading actress in the film and the woman who'd funded the project—knew that she wanted her movie to be a stylized comedy. Since I had a musical theatre background, I suggested that we make it a musical comedy. She liked the idea, so we hired a composer and choreographer. Of course, when I say "hire," I mean we paid them a few hundred dollars, max. Unfortunately, a $35,000 budget does not allow much wiggle room when the majority of the cash goes to the cost of film, development, and equipment. For the most part, we had to inspire people to be a part of the project by showing them how special we knew it could be—more special, in a sense, than dollars. Wonderfully, some of the amazing people involved in *The Boy Scout* came on board, including our production designer, Nicole, and our cinematographer, Ken.

Annie and I had been working together to find a director for the project, and one day when she and I were talking about the film over a meal, she suggested that I fill that role. With a big smile on my face, I agreed. Back in college, I tried directing and was clueless; this time, I had a strong vision about the timing, the dialogue, the music, the dancing, and the look of the film.

Pre-production was a whirlwind of three or four months. After some difficulty finding a set, we ended up renting a house in Burbank for a month. A week before filming began, we were transforming the house into the home of our main character, Gretchen. One of our producers had a family in the landscaping business, so he completely landscaped the front yard, adding new flowers and sod, making it look fresh and inviting. On the inside, every room got a new coat of bright paint under Nicole's meticulous fingers. Then we moved in furniture we had rented from a prop house and actualized a universe of five or six different rooms, which was a far bigger project than the one stylized room in *The Boy Scout*.

When I remember *Gretchen Brettschneider Skirts Thirty*, I'm struck by the magnificent job Nicole did in choosing colors. Gretchen's bedroom was bright green, and all of the accents were pink. The phone had eyeballs and lips on it. There were headshot pictures on the wall of Gretchen's best friends, one of whom was dressed in blue, one in yellow, and one in green, and the photos were hung on the wall vertically like a column. Everything had its place. Nicole put the room together in a way that was beautifully childlike, even though it belonged to a twenty-nine-year-old woman.

It was exciting to play in that environment, when so many things were coming together on set, and everyone on the crew was either volunteering or working for a fraction of their traditional rate because they believed in the project. It was a powerful and inspiring feeling, especially when the product looked better than I had imagined it could. To bring a universe to life creatively is more magical than I can describe.

After we built the set, we had to think logistics: setting up a side room for make-up; placing chairs and tables in the backyard for dining; creating a holding room for actors who were not filming; determining the times that traffic and airport noise were the loudest. I immensely enjoyed this new way of thinking—this logical, meticulous side of directing I didn't know existed.

On days when we had production meetings, I would get to Annie's condo, where we'd meet an hour before the crew arrived. I'd bring a couple bags of groceries and make pancakes and soufflés and muffins and have fruit, juice, and coffee waiting. There was a family element of people coming together for a big meal and enjoying one another's company. But there was also something special about serving the crew—the people who were working for us—because after that meal, I would be asking a lot from them, and I was going to be serious and candid about what I needed. Nourishment was my way of respecting the crew's contribution to the film.

Those meetings made me feel alive because they were so full of potential. Eight or ten department heads sat around a big table, reporting on what they'd accomplished and what they were offering to the project, relaying their vision, and listening to one another. Everybody genuinely cared. Indeed, some of the people working with us were making five or ten times as much money at other industry jobs, but I always hoped that on our project, they felt as though they were part of a dream and that the camaraderie would compensate them on an emotional level. It was an intense environment and one in which, I think, anyone who hadn't brought their complete best would have felt like they had failed the rest of us.

In that kind of atmosphere, it was frustrating when little things went wrong, like a producer showing up to a rehearsal with a great meal for fifteen people but without utensils or napkins. When you're trying to respect people who are donating their time and you're on a time-crunch yourself, incidents like that can have a big impact on a schedule and on attitudes. It was the difference between inspiring people to take the extra step versus giving in to bits of carelessness.

When we filmed *Gretchen,* we were trying to shoot three or four pages in a day—and we spent four or five months prior to that with a team of fifteen or more people preparing for those days. The attention to detail, the care and nurturance that went into every scene, every moment, was phenomenal.

In the end, the film was adorable. We rehearsed the timing of the choreography and pre-recorded the music in a sound studio so we could dance with it on a click track. I realized that I had failed at directing in college because I was too scared to dive in, but I immersed myself in this film at all levels. It was fun, ludicrous, silly. But it was not unstructured silliness; it was rehearsed silliness.

In one scene, Gretchen is chased around by a giant orange foam "30" as her three best friends in their brightly colored 20s costumes and slicked-back hair are cheering for her with pom-poms. In another scene, we're performing synchronized swimming in the pool. The lead actress is in red, and I'm in green shorts and a green swimming cap. It was absolutely ridiculous but so rich and unique. We had taken Annie's idea, which could have been poorly executed, and made it special. There was no doubt about that.

The first screening of *Gretchen* was different from the one for *The Boy Scout*. Because *The Boy Scout* had been the first, there was an incredible high in seeing the audience love it and a kind of disbelief that we had *done* it. For *Gretchen*, the audience response was more of a reassurance. I remember when John from the original Elevation 9000 approached me after the screening. I respected his opinion, and when he told me that I'd "done it again," the acknowledgment was powerful and launched me again into that zone where I felt invincible.

The film ended up being one that kids wanted to watch over and over again. My mother was a nanny for six-year-old twins who probably watched the movie more than a hundred times. Every time they saw my mother, they'd beg, "Can we watch Gretchen? Can we watch Gretchen?" I saw one of the twins again recently, five or six years after the movie was made, and he *still* asked me about Gretchen! The marketing person in me knew (and still knows) that the movie's concept was a gem. It was an adult story about being terrified of your thirtieth birthday and of losing your youth, and yet it captured the young, much like *Bugs Bunny* did despite its adult themes and content.

So, just like *The Boy Scout*, *Gretchen* was an exceptional concept that we fully executed. But, like an idiot, I followed in the footsteps of many other directors and started dating Annie. I love people enough to begin with, but I tend to have intense feelings for people with whom I share the creative process. In *Gretchen,* I was both working physically close to Annie and also guiding her on an emotional journey. It was easy for me to confuse caring for her vision with the desire to build a romantic relationship.

During the filming of the movie, people started talking. Our crewmembers and fellow actors knew that Annie and I had started some kind of relationship, and that knowledge was influencing the way they looked at the project. When things were going great, they couldn't have cared less who was dating whom, but when things were going less successfully, speculation as to *why* was rampant. And that negativity spread like a fever. For me, as the director, knowing that people were gossiping and speculating about why things weren't going as well one hour as they were an hour earlier—well, it was brutal: an end-of-the-world kind of pressure after the incredible high of building a universe that *worked*. Watching that universe fall apart around me in those moments was like watching a house I'd built collapse on my head. Still, I had to remain focused. I knew that if I started frustrating Annie because of my own anxiety about the situation, her performance could suffer.

Well, in the end, it was the *future* of the project that suffered most. Because I crossed professional boundaries, Annie felt used—and confused—unsure what my motives had been from the beginning. She protected herself from further heartache by becoming cold to me, which I deserved. Meanwhile, my judgment had again come into question with the crew, and rightfully so.

After months of battling it out with Annie, I released all of my interest in the project for a small sum, and I walked away with everybody hating one another … again. To my knowledge, Annie didn't do much with that film other than bury it in the closet and move on with her life. I had no choice but to do the same.

#J^UMP 4

NAÏVETÉ

AFTER we finished filming *Gretchen,* but before Annie started hating my guts, we wanted to publicize the premiere. Because we recognized that the best way to draw attention was to help somebody, we decided to make the premiere a fundraiser for the Make-A-Wish Foundation. We chose The Ivar, a big, beautiful Hollywood club, as our venue. Mark Thompson, a well-known radio personality, all around awesome guy, and fellow actor at Playhouse West was our emcee.

Though I don't remember exactly how many people were at the premiere, I recall stuffing a thousand gift bags before the event. We'd gotten several sponsors, so we filled the bags with magazines, a copy of the movie, and other goodies. We also had a painting made by a phenomenal actor we'd gone to acting school with, a Texas artist named Brady Smith, who has a unique, Southwestern style. He made a huge welcome sign for the event with elements from the movie, and we auctioned off this painting and several other items for the benefit of Make-A-Wish.

#JUMP

The premiere was cool, complete with red carpet, photographers, and celebrities. Through the auction, we raised somewhere between six and eight thousand dollars for Make-A-Wish. It wasn't a ton of money, but the foundation was appreciative. Afterward, they approached me with a special request. They had a Make-A-Wish child whose wish they had been trying to grant for years and wondered if I could help.

This particular girl suffered from a cavernous angioma at the base of her skull as a toddler; essentially, she'd had a series of debilitating strokes as an infant. It was a miracle that she made it through them, but she spent the next several years learning to crawl and then walk again. Those years were incredibly difficult for her family. Their insurance coverage capped out at a million dollars and her father sold his wedding ring to help pay additional medical bills before the family lost their house and was eventually forced to claim bankruptcy.

When we met the little girl, she was ten or eleven and no longer in immediate danger. Although the family had healed itself to some degree, it was still debilitated as a result of the tragedy. There were two other kids in the family; one was this girl's twin and one was their younger brother. So much attention had been paid to the little girl because of her illness that the others were neglected. Still, they were all trying to love each other and do the best they could under the circumstances, and our group found them to be an amazing family.

Because of all her strokes, the little girl's face was partially paralyzed, and it was hard for her to talk. She could use her tongue but not her lips, so she would push her tongue against the side of her mouth in order to speak. Despite her difficulties, she had a bright spirit and big dreams. Her wish was to be a star. And the best way to do that, she felt, was to tell her story.

With Jesse and David, two producers who had been integral in getting *Gretchen* made, I started on a half-hour documentary about the little girl's life. I worked closely with David, who was directing the documentary. He was a guy with whom I could be authentic because we had the same core values, and our partnership on this project felt natural (David would eventually become the VP of Round Table).

For the filming, we all went to the family's house and made breakfast with them, much like we had done on *Gretchen*. Afterwards, we recorded and interviewed different family members and attended some of the little girl's rehabilitation sessions, such as when she had equine therapy. She also wanted to be a dancer, so we filmed her in her small dance studio at home. Her coordination was less than perfect, but her spirit—her desire—was beautiful.

My wife Dawn (then my fiancée) lent a lot to my understanding of the situation. Dawn is a psychologist and helped me understand what a child with special needs might be going through growing up in a normal world. On a trip to visit me in L.A. (she lived in Chicago), Dawn helped us ask some provocative questions about how the little girl had been affected by her illness and what she now thought about life. After all, the girl was growing up. She was entering puberty and was being made fun of at school for her disabilities. What must coping with all that have been like for her?

After filming, the interviews were transcribed, and Dave and I scripted them together. Finally, Dave hired an editor to piece together the documentary. When it was finished, we had a red-carpet premiere at The Grove, a huge outdoor

#JUMP

shopping center and theater in Hollywood. The little girl got to ride in a limo up to the red carpet, and Fox News was there to capture it all. It was an amazing moment for her, and I felt honored to have been involved. Sadly, at the same time, her parents' marriage was falling apart. I couldn't blame them. It was incredible that they'd weathered the storm that long.

The whole project took about five or six moths. The Make-A-Wish Foundation paid us a small amount (basically returning to us the money we'd raised for them at the *Gretchen* premiere), which helped offset expenses. But we didn't do it for money or to draw attention to anyone but the little girl. We were making a difference in her life, and that felt good—especially after I had fallen so hard after jumping into both of my previous film projects.

A few month's later, Dave called to tell me that the little girl's mother had committed suicide. I recently heard that her death was later reclassified as cardiac arrest, because it was unclear exactly how she passed. At the time, thinking she had taken her own life was a stunning turn of events that opened my eyes to the pain some people face in overcoming obstacles. I had been naïve enough to believe that our creative process might combat the sadness and drama of this family's ordeal, that we could play a role in helping them recover from the trauma of the little girl's illness. The mother's suicide was a brass-knuckled fist to my gut: I was not able to solve all of life's problems. I was not even able to come close, and that pissed me off at first and then just made me terribly sad. Almost like I thought I had jumped with great integrity, but was now trapped in a cold free-fall.

#J^UMP 5

INNER PAIN REACHING OUT

AFTER *Gretchen* fell apart, I retreated into mourning again, the way I did when *The Boy Scout* and Elevation 9000 failed. I was as low as I'd ever been, beginning to seriously doubt my ability to actualize my dreams. I was also privately blaming everyone around me, and the world itself, for not seeing that my intentions were good, and for not giving a damn about the nice, fun, adorable movies I'd made. In short, it was the perfect time for someone to approach me and say, *Hey! I want to give a big 'F--- you' to an audience! You wanna play?*

My response?

Suuuure!

It was 2004, and despite pouring my soul into my film projects, I was still making a living from commercials and TV appearances. However, I was so disenchanted with the experience of going out on auditions that I was starting to

#JUMP

make less money: I didn't want to be there, so I was caring less and therefore doing a mediocre job when I was on set. Meanwhile, when I wasn't working, I was getting high in an effort to avoid my depression. I had parted ways with Chris and Brad and all things related to Elevation 9000, and started working more with David and Jesse, my new partners in crime. Together, we created the LA Film Lab, an extension of the Elevation 9000 Film Lab idea, where we worked with people to develop their ideas, while looking for a couple of projects we could produce.

With this new movie project, I would give the audience something I'd never done before, something that would make them feel awful—truly awful—about the world. Then I'd see how they reacted. It wasn't a conscious decision, but that is exactly how it played out.

The movie was called *Unsuitable*. It was the true story of a woman who had been a prima ballerina before a car accident crushed her, destroying her body. After the accident, she went from being a petite, strong, beautiful dancer to a depressed and overweight woman who didn't take care of herself. The destruction of this woman's dreams didn't end with the car accident. Afterward, she got engaged to a man who brutally raped her. As a result of it all, she was unhappy, mean, and smoked like a chimney—but the woman wanted her story told and had the money to make it happen. And I needed to finance my next leap.

I saw the film as an opportunity, and maybe that was what allowed me to push back my discomfort at the woman's aim—to make the audience feel like she did in life: crippled. She felt like a victim and believed that life was nasty and that other people needed to see just how nasty it could be. I'd experienced disappointments and failures, but I had not had my dreams ripped from me the way she had, and I had never been sexually abused; to be in a situation where I could explore these dark parts of the human experience was foreign and fascinating to me. I didn't have the wisdom to realize how negative an impact a project like this would have on my psyche.

Against the odds, some of the people I'd worked with on *The Boy Scout* and Gretchen worked with me again on *Unsuitable*. I was now intimately familiar with directing, in all of its joys and heartbreaks. The amount of preparation and care that goes into a film, all of the rehearsal, all of the perfection you're aiming for, all of the questions asked before the camera starts rolling, the forty-five people staring at you to perform and get it right so you can all move on … It's incredible pressure. Awesome pressure. Fun pressure. Exciting pressure. Terrifying pressure. And when you don't get it right and you have to move on anyway, it's desperate pressure. I felt like a genius when everything was going right but a complete and total incompetent bastard when it wasn't.

As director, I made sure we took just as much care to create the universe of this film as we had with the previous ones. We rented and painted a loft in downtown L.A., and commissioned an artist to paint a beautiful picture of a dancing couple that we hung above the main character's bed on the set. The imagery of the film was dark and moody, and we hired a fantastic choreographer named Michelle Zeitlin, and cast professional dancers. We knew that the soundtrack would be an equally powerful component to the actors' emotional journey, so we were thrilled when Tom McRae, an amazing musician and UK phenomenon, agreed to let us use his music for the film. I would listen to his songs over and over again through preproduction. They were dark, passionate, and sometimes beautifully angry. In fact, the film was almost built like an extended music video where, intermingled with the woman's current life, there were haunting visual images from her past—dancing scenes that were romantic and emotional. Exquisite.

Ken, my director of photography on the previous films, filmed this beautiful dancing. He used grainy 8 mm film and juxtaposed it with the clarity of 35 mm film, which we used to shoot the woman's current life: She is miserable and lonely, fighting for attention and wanting her fiancé to change her life. But while she's looking forward to her wedding, her fiancé is writing a book and does not have the emotional capacity to care for her wounds and victimization. The contrast was stark—the beauty of her past versus the reality of her present. But the story ends with a scene where the couple is viciously fighting. Then, when her fiancé finds out that she slept with an old boyfriend who returned to her life, he takes ultimate control over her and rapes her. We pushed our limits with this scene. It goes on too long and is horribly uncomfortable (probably quite realistic) ... and the movie ends on that note. So, as the audience, you're seeing the lead-in and trying to figure out whether this couple is going to make it and then there's this explosive, traumatizing ending, and that's IT! I felt as though the movie left people like open carcasses, as if we were saying, "Thanks for coming, hope you don't bleed too much on your way out."

Like the woman whose story I was telling, I also felt like a victim at this point in my life. We were both two-dimensional in that regard, and that created a lack of accountability in the characters we wrote. *Unsuitable* was the first time I had participated in the writing of a script, and I know that my own feelings of bitterness contributed to my doing a less than stellar writing job. The recognition that the writing was not where I wanted it to be was part of what led me to ultimately found a writing company in subsequent years.

Still, in some ways, *Unsuitable* worked, and it was powerful to have created an emotional drama, which was so different from my previous work. I think I achieved what this woman wanted, and we got beautiful write-ups in *Dance Spirit Magazine* and *Hollywood Screenwriter*. We got good publicity. We even tried to partner with Rape, Abuse & Incest National Network (RAINN) in hopes that the organization could use the film to inspire people to talk about their experiences, but it didn't go anywhere. I can certainly imagine why RAINN didn't want to use the film: it didn't end well.

Despite the movie's arguable promise, I realized quickly that I hated it. I hated feeling like I was abusing the audience. It was torturous to know that the production value of the project was so good that it demanded respect, and that the dancing was beautiful, but that the writing and the characters lacked the depth they required to take people on the kind of journey I wanted to create. At the end of the day, we subjected our audience to such ugliness without deserving their attention, which made it gratuitous. In storytelling, robbing the audience of a fulfilling resolution is risky, and I don't imagine this was a case where people walked away wanting to discuss the film and explore what may have happened after the final scene. I can't imagine a group of friends sitting around a table and asking one another over cocktails, "How do you think it ended? Did they get back together?" Instead, it was something they wanted to forget. It was something *I* wanted to forget.

I decided then that I would never again lend my time to something that made people feel badly about life or the world. I wonder what those who knew me thought as they watched me go from *The Boy Scout's* bright spirit to this bitter, ugly, crybaby part of myself. Now, years later, I think that making this film was my cry for help. Instead of directly articulating how confused I felt about how Hollywood was changing me, I expressed myself in my work. And when I saw myself up on that screen, I was disgusted. Something had to change soon, or I would be in real trouble.

#J^UMP 6

MISMATCHED VALUES

AT the same time we were filming *Unsuitable*, I was working on another project called *Redirect* that Jesse was directing for LA Film Lab. Even after producing it, being on set every day and watching it on film multiple times—even with the clarity of hindsight—I still couldn't tell you what it was about. I think that Jesse wanted to create a film that didn't make linear sense but was interesting. He loved the idea of keeping people's attention while asking them to fill in many of the blanks left in the storytelling. That vision excited him.

What I *can* tell you about the film is that there was a heist involved. There was also a death and gunplay and stunts involving people scaling over the sides of buildings. We had professional cops on set because we were using real guns, and a Hollywood stunt team helped us with the rappelling and fight scenes. Making this film should have been so interesting, so fun—but it was rough on me.

Jesse was a doer: results-driven, hard working, and all about logistics. He had recently helped me on *Unsuitable*, where our roles had been reversed: I had been the director while he had served as producer.

One day, on *Unsuitable*, we were on set and I was having difficulty concentrating. People were goofing around in the dance studio we had created for the film, and I needed to make some important decisions. As the director, I finally said, "Can everyone please quiet down?"

Jesse turned to me. His voice was scathing when he said, "People need to let off steam. They're working hard for you."

Made in front of everybody, the comment was instantly disempowering. I felt like the butt of a joke. I called him aside to talk and let him know I was upset by his approach to dealing with me. He responded defensively and with no apologies.

After that incident, I was already knee-deep in production for *Redirect*, which we would soon be filming. We were entrenched, and though I was offended by what had happened on *Unsuitable*, I put my head down and went to work for him. As his producer, I was responsible for helping actualize his vision. As director, he was the leader of an army that was going to battle for a number of days. I thought, *Okay, now you'll feel what the pressure is like and how beneficial it is to have supportive colleagues around you*. Yes, I was bratty. I know!

The preparation for filming—the production process—was challenging, but everyone had great attitudes. Then when we got on set, it became immediately obvious that he and I had different approaches to filmmaking. Jesse believed that the best way to take care of people involved in a project is to produce a great result. I believed—and still do—that if you take care of your people, they will take care of your project. On other sets, I had watched directors worry about their product and not their people, and I always felt disconnected. People often wanted to get through such projects, collect their paycheck or their resume credit, and move on. That's not the kind of environment that, to me, is conducive to great work or a creative journey. I was unprepared to take on a leadership role where I could not exert my own approach to people—yet there I was. Capable of providing big-picture input but not ultimately in charge. I wasn't the director, and it wasn't my money.

One day, one of the lead actors on *Redirect* called in and told us that he had another opportunity and wouldn't be coming in that day. Now, *Redirect* was a small project, but about $50,000 was invested in four days of filming. The majority of the funds were spent on equipment and film, which, again, didn't leave much for cast and crew. A lot of people were either volunteering their time or working for low rates. An actor not showing up was a HUGE issue.

After that phone call, Jesse appeared to shut down for a while, which was understandable—this would impact the film greatly. He didn't know whether we should call off filming for the day or resume without the lead actor. As most of the funding for the project had come from a loan that Jesse and the lead actress had taken out, I had little say about our next moves. So I waited for Jesse.

So did the rest of the crew.

For hours, cast and crew sat around while Jesse figured out what direction he wanted to take. That wasn't the end of the world, but when he finally made his decision, he expected everyone to put in a full day beyond the time they'd already spent there. It went from being a scheduled twelve-hour day to an anticipated fifteen- or sixteen-hour day (which probably meant eighteen hours). And he did it without gathering everyone together and saying, "Look, I know this is rough, but I need you guys here." There was none of that. Just expectation. That disappointed and embarrassed me, as I felt it was a poor reflection of our group and a poor reflection of me as a producer.

What is still hard for me is that I like Jesse so much. He's a good guy and smart. But I didn't like working for him. I didn't want to rally the troops for him, and in that regard, I failed at my job, and, on a personal level, I failed my friend. There were pockets of conversation going on between filming, where groups of three or four would complain to one another. People were pulling me aside and saying, "This isn't right." Because I had worked with many of these people before, they trusted me and were trying to push me to solve a problem that I didn't know how to solve.

I think what upset me most was that, on that particular day of filming, we used the home of the Make-A-Wish family we had helped. Jesse had been an instrumental part of that project by helping produce it, and he had maintained communication with the family afterward. When he asked them if we could use their home as a set for *Redirect*, naturally, they agreed. They were grateful for what we had done for their little girl.

So, compounding the issue of how I felt about the crew being disrespected was the length of time we spent in this family's home. For all those hours, forty-five or so people traipsed through their house with heavy equipment. And present the whole time were the three young children—the twelve-year-old twins and eight-year-old boy. I felt as though we were taking advantage of them. As though we were asking for recompense for the nice thing we had done for their family.

The whole situation made me feel trapped and angry. The best thing I could do was lead by example, as much as I could: stay positive, put in long hours, and work hard. But it was all a ruse, and I probably didn't mask my frustration nearly as well as I hoped. Indeed, I probably undermined Jesse because I disagreed with his choice to push the crew without their buy-in.

I think, now, that what I saw in Jesse's treatment of his crew and audience was a direct reflection of my own actions with *Unsuitable*. Through that movie, I had created a vehicle for my bitterness and set it loose on my audience, under the pretense of delivering them a piece of "art." Jesse took advantage of his audience in a different way, an audacious, straightforward way. He wasn't trying to hide his intentions like I had. That was part of why this experience was so difficult for me: It showed me yet another part of myself I didn't like and that I couldn't respect. I was willing to use an audience for my own end, under the ever-present veil of good intentions.

At the end of the day, Jesse and I didn't share the same leadership approach, and that gap made working together challenging when the heat was turned up. Fortunately, though, I had learned yet another powerful lesson. Similar to my experience on *Unsuitable*, when I realized what kind of content I wanted to produce, *Redirect* taught me that I will never work for another person, another leader, whose approach doesn't more directly align with my own. It also forced me to start the process of being honest with myself about who I was becoming and what my desire for Hollywood success was doing to me.

PART II

A CHANGE IN SCENERY

… #J^UMP 7

TOO MUCH A BUSINESSMAN

AFTER all I had now been through, I was both disenchanted and disengaged with the Los Angeles experience. Just as I'd been doing since shortly after *Gretchen*, I was smoking a lot of pot to avoid the reality that I didn't know what was happening to my dream. Would it ever be actualized the way I'd imagined for so many years? At the same time, a number of my other close friends had graduated to harder drugs, and our relationships were changing drastically and quickly. I was also seriously dating my soon-to-be wife Dawn, who had gotten in touch with me after seeing one of my commercials on television. (To give you an idea of how arrogant I still was around that time, despite my fears and failed jumps, my response to her contacting me was, "Look who comes out of the woodwork when you're on TV." How she didn't flip me the bird and run is beyond me. I give her a lot of credit—and she likes credit!)

#JUMP

In any case, after filming *Unsuitable*, I was honest with Dawn about how much I was smoking. As a school psychologist in Chicago, she worked with kids and families that have been torn apart by drugs, and she knew from these experiences that pot is frequently the gateway to more dangerous behaviors. Understandably, she had a zero-tolerance for smoking. She said, "You're going to stop, or we're going to stop." I quit pot cold turkey right then and never looked back. I quit cigarettes at the same time, cleaning up my act fast, and that transition was startling for me. I had to face real life in a way that I hadn't ever been required to do.

One of our first major decisions as a serious couple was to figure out where we were going to live. Dawn said she would move out to L.A., and there was a part of me that was attracted to that possibility. I thought, *If she loves me, she'll support my dreams; I can still chase all this.* Then there was another part of me that thought, *Grow up!* That part of me also wanted a more stable income. What I had been doing all those years—making films—hadn't been about money, about profit. It had all been about passion, about possibility. I was still being compensated here and there by commercial work, but I knew that I needed to figure out how to make money in a way that was reliable.

During this time, I was starting to make longer trips to Chicago, living with Dawn in the city for three or four weeks at a time. During those trips, I began focusing more on writing. I had co-written *Unsuitable*, and though I recognized that I was no brilliant writer, I enjoyed the process and recognized that I needed to learn how to be a better writer in order to be a well-rounded artist.

I started exploring a website on which individuals and companies posted projects and invited freelance writers to bid. There were all kinds of projects that I could not do because they required myriad areas of expertise: technology, health and fitness, beauty, medical, etc. Something clicked in me, and I thought, *What if I put together a group of writers who can do all these things, and I'll manage them and take care of the customers?* So I found a writer who could do something I couldn't do, bid on an appropriate project, paid the writer, and took a percentage of the revenue. The writer was happy and the client was happy. Slowly, I started repeating the process, and it was making me money.

What I found was that I could perform a service that both the clients and the writers found difficult: communicating. The writers didn't know how to *hear* what a client needed, while the clients didn't know how to articulate what they needed. I thought, *Wow! I can provide an intermediary experience where I take care of both the writer and the client, and ensure that they each get what they need to drive the desired result.* And I can get paid to do it.

I had never created anything from the perspective of making money. I had been happy eating peanut butter and jelly sandwiches as long as I could pay my cheap rent and be creative. Now, I felt as though I was making free money by leveraging other people's expertise. In a sense, I undervalued what I was good at, and it took some time for me to realize that communication is a valuable skill for which it is okay to be compensated.

I think that realization was what led to me escalating the game. It was probably late 2005, and I had been bidding on projects and managing client-writer relationships for about six months. I liked working with writers. I liked editing their work, taking a client's need and delivering something better than he or she had envisioned. In April 2006, I incorporated

#JUMP

Writers of the Round Table Inc.—and that forced me to think of my work from a different angle. A business angle.

Despite feeling as though the idea *itself* was creative, managing my new business didn't feel creative on a daily basis. I was using more of my head than my heart, thinking strategically: how would I find more clients and more writers, and communicate to each what the other needed? I had to wear a full-on business cap for the first time, and I was fumbling my way through. I had never taken a business course or thought about being a businessperson; I just liked people and had this skill that neither the writers nor clients seemed to be strong in.

As I repeated the process of bidding for projects and assigning them to the writer best suited to them, I kept myself open to opportunity: When I came across a talented writer, I would assess what his or her skills were and then go out and try to sell a service based on those abilities. If I had a good writer who loved writing about healthcare, for example, I'd go after healthcare clients. If I found a writer who excelled in penning articles for women, I searched out magazines that wanted to hire them. And the whole time, I was amazed that it was *working*. I was making money, enough to pay my bills and get married; even if it wasn't lavish, the wedding was beautiful and intimate.

I felt as though I was on the right path, but I also realized that I felt a loneliness I had not experienced before. The loneliness was not for a lack of other people around me; it was because I had cast aside the part of myself that I enjoyed so much: the creative. Desperate to build a life away from L.A. and the heartbreak I had experienced there, I had swung my pendulum so far in the other direction that I felt stale—bored with myself. The process I was creating inspired me and exercised my artistic side, but the products I was delivering to clients didn't move me; I wasn't passionate about the latest innovation in healthcare or how a piece of software worked. Instead, just as I'd always been, I was more interested in people who wanted to share personal stories. That gap had me feeling depressed much of the time. Intellectually I was being stimulated, but I knew that my business needed a heart center and I had yet to find it. And there it was: for the first time in my working life, I was positioned to find the balance between business and creativity.

#JUMP 8

PROFESSIONAL BOUNDARIES

ANGELICA Harris was an author I had been working with for some time as a side project. As part of LA Film Lab in L.A., I had been preparing to teach an online screenwriting course and made it a point to chat with people in writing groups to spread the word for the course and attract potential participants. That was when I met Angelica.

She was working on an Arthurian legend piece at the time that was epic in scope. I've always loved films about medieval magic and sorcery and knights, so the project appealed to me. But Angelica was not a screenwriter; she was a novelist.

We continued communicating, and I asked her to send me a copy of the first book in her Arthurian series. I could tell from the level of detail in it that she had a great sense of imagination, and it was obvious that she loved researching the time period. Both were awesome characteristics. However, when it came to the vision for the story and understanding how the reader was experiencing it on the page, Angelica needed support.

As I read her material, it was easy to see how and where I could augment the novel. For example, one of my major concerns was that the characters all sounded the same—and shallow characters are not easily cared for by readers. At that point, Angelica's second book was about to go to print, and she had me edit a portion of it before sending it to press. She may have expected me to tell her it was good to go, but instead, I gave her a wake-up call. She needed to make a crucial decision: was she going to print the book on schedule, despite seeing the value of my suggestions, or was she going to go back and rewrite the entire book with me? She decided to print it, but she hired me to help her write the third book in the series.

Angelica had just begun working on her next novel, and it was the first book project I'd ever taken part in. For many reasons, the process was arduous. First, it was a difficult story to develop—rich in thematic content, imagination, and detail. Angelica excelled in these things, but she still consistently struggled to translate the vivid, breathtaking story in her mind to words on the page. The writing rambled, making it hard for readers to experience the story the way she did, the way the story deserved to be experienced. She had a powerful message, and it could have been so easily lost. As a result, we were constantly in a state of rewriting, even as we moved forward. Fortunately, Angelica was a pro who took her whippings from me and continually dove back into the work.

A bigger issue that arose challenged me both personally and professionally. Angelica is an emotional person, and the tortured souls in her books are a reflection of her own life.

She'd had a tough upbringing and had been forced to overcome many obstacles, including being nearly beaten to death by her mother on multiple occasions. We enjoyed a close working relationship, but I sometimes felt Angelica was trying to use me as a therapist. In candid discussions, she would share with me some of her personal problems.

In my own desire to be liked/loved, I would listen, sometimes for hours, thinking that was the appropriate way to care for her. Eventually, I would try to pull her back to the topic of her writing, but it was difficult to navigate between the role of emotional supporter and my professional role. I never wanted to hurt her feelings in the short term but failed to realize that by not setting firm boundaries, I was contributing to her being "stuck" in a victim mentality. Finally learning to set those boundaries took years for me. Over time, I learned that the more I set boundaries, the more she produced results. When she didn't have me as an outlet for her personal life, she got back to doing her work, and ultimately, her work changed her life.

In all, the process of writing Angelica's book took five years. We ended up with a novel of about eight hundred pages, which we decided to split into two books, *Excalibur Reclaims Her King* and the fourth, as yet unpublished, book in the series.

Those years of working with Angelica taught me an important lesson: that I am most helpful to my clients when I push them creatively rather than coddle their personal fears. Because of my experiences growing up, when I was taught to avoid angering or upsetting people, my first instinct is often to say yes to my clients. But for Angelica, I was most nurturing when I was persistent with the tough commentary, when I asked her to keep her personal problems out of our

#J**UMP**

work together, when I pushed her to go back and constantly rework the novel rather than accept what she had already written.

Today, though Angelica is older than me, she is like a younger sister I have watched grow up and then helped push out of the nest. Five years of creating this story together was an intense adventure. I'm incredibly proud of her and even more so since she has finished her personal memoir *Living with Rage* edited by our own Katie Gutierrez Painter. Finally stepping out from behind her fictional characters Angelica is now sharing her own story and its a masterpiece that we're confident will impact lives on a massive scale (the book was released December 2011).

Since 2009, Angelica has also been building a reading program that's garnering great reactions from the state of New York. She loves working with children and inspiring them to read, and working with women who have experienced abuse, inspiring them to take control of their lives. She has been invited to speak all over the state, and the media has been paying attention to her non-profit, The Excalibur Reading Program. All along, she's had wonderful intentions, the right intentions, but she also needed to stop feeling like a victim and mature in order for the right people to take her seriously enough to help her achieve her dreams. Hmm … Sounds a lot like me.

#J^UMP 9

TRAILBLAZING

BEA Fields is an executive coach, a provocative woman in that she doesn't like to mess around. When she and I started communicating in 2006, she knew exactly what she wanted: to produce a book that would push the envelope in her industry. Even before we spoke, she knew she wanted to do this through storytelling. No traditional business book for her.

My relationship with Bea started out flawlessly, with ease. On one of our first phone calls, she told me about her career. She had always been known for pushing the limits, and she wanted this book to be no different. Bea was, in other words, the perfect marriage of what I'd been doing for Writers of the Round Table—which was so business-oriented—and my past career in storytelling. Since she was so forthright about her ideas and objectives, I was quickly able to build a story arc for her book. Thrilled, she said, "Bingo! You got it."

What would become *Edge! A Leadership Story* was a traditional hero's journey. A struggling CEO comes into contact with a character who is, essentially, Bea. The CEO, desperate to turn his company around, is forced by his board of directors to work with this executive coach. He fights it hard for a while, and then buys into the idea of an executive coach in *mind* but doesn't invest his heart in it. He goes through a series of lazy attempts to engage in her process, and as a result of his half-hearted efforts, his company continues to sink. Finally, the CEO realizes that he needs to invest his whole self in the process. That's when the good work starts, as do the real results. Under the Bea-character's guidance, the CEO turns his company in a successful new direction and learns some powerful lessons about himself in the process.

Bea, who dearly values transparency, knew that she would credit the people who worked with her on the project. She wasn't interested in hiring a ghostwriter and trying to convince people that she was a brilliant storyteller or writer. She wanted to be seen as an expert for what she does: helping leaders become more successful. Bea also liked the idea of partnering with people who were smart and successful in their own industries. I think she liked demonstrating that she was somebody who knew how to surround herself with the right people for the job. I had a clear picture of the story, but felt it needed a different writing style than my own, so we engaged Eva Silva as the writer and got to work.

The writing process took more than a year, during which we consistently met our goals for the project. The first of these goals was to flesh out the characters as much as possible. Bea would do mock guidance phone calls with another coach, the awesome Roger DeWitt. Roger would play the CEO, while Bea became Kate Nelson, the executive coach in the book. Roger happens to have been a Broadway actor prior to his coaching career, so these calls felt authentic. They allowed us a juicy glimpse of how Bea works in real time and helped us strengthen and define Kate as a character. In total, Bea and Roger did about a dozen of these calls, and the recordings served as a basis for the work Bea's character did on the weekly phone calls with her client in the book.

The journey was alive throughout that year. It was joyful. Bea enjoyed the creative process and trusted our expertise, so the collaboration was comfortable and fluid. We built the book chapter by chapter, laughing as we discovered our characters and their humanity, all the while rooting for our CEO hero, Mitch, to get in the game and step up to the plate. I distinctly remember a series of phone calls where we read the chapters aloud together, named each one, and then discussed the lesson being lived out. We used these discussions to form what we called the end-of-chapter "debriefs," which presented each chapter's lessons to readers in ways they could use within their own businesses and lives.

I loved the approach and was so proud of the book. I had seen other business parables but none that used such in-depth character development—and certainly none that took the reader on such an emotional and intimate journey. We were ready to show this to the world.

Thus began the writing of the book proposal and query letters, a traditional approach to finding an agent who loved the book enough to champion it and sell it to a publisher. We invested about three months in creating the first version of the proposal, and, again, we were proud of it. So off it went to agents.

Almost every time, we received strong feedback. People liked the concept. Thought it was a good book. But they didn't think they could sell it because nothing like it existed in the marketplace. No one would take the chance. The book belonged in the business section, but these agents didn't have faith that a character-driven story, a narrative journey, would sell there. There was no track record for such a thing.

So, despite every agent out there clamoring for something new and fresh, our book was so new and fresh that it scared them away from touching it. It was like Hollywood rejection all over again, but this time I felt as though I had dragged Bea with me, and I was pissed off at myself for not being able to make her dream a reality. Somehow we had to get this book out.

After exhausting other avenues, we followed a recommendation to go with a company that referred to itself as an "entrepreneurial publisher." It seemed like a great match for us, and Bea and I flew to New York to meet with the owner of the company. The owner was kind, and the publishing contract mentioned a lot of a support, so Bea made the decision to move forward.

The first step was for Bea to pay the publisher for the book cover and interior design, as well as for a slew of other promises related to marketing the book. Bea also agreed that the company would take eighty percent of the proceeds from book sales, a lower percentage than what a traditional commercial publisher would have taken. It seemed reasonable for the level of professionalism and support we thought we would be getting from the company.

While we were finishing *Edge!*, Bea decided to use the publisher for another book we were helping her with: *Millennial Leaders*. A more straightforward business book based on interviews Bea had recorded with twenty-five young entrepreneurs, *Millennial Leaders* was put on an expedited timeline because Bea was due to speak at a major event in L.A., for which she wanted the book ready. The publisher said no problem.

That was when the problems began.

First, we hated all the cover concepts the publisher delivered to us. The concepts were horrific and the process confusing. The publisher seemed insulted, but the team put together a few more options. Still, we were dissatisfied, so Bea hired an independent designer who put together a killer cover. Then we began the company's publishing process. The communication was terrible—we eventually found out that a college intern had been put in charge of our account: someone with little to no experience in publishing, who was not prepared to work with an aggressive duo like Bea and me.

The problems with *Millennial Leaders* carried over to our work with *Edge*. Quickly, we were coming to realize that this company had taken Bea's money with no intention of doing anything more than printing her book and charging her exorbitantly for it. My education about vanity publishers was coming hard and fast. Such firms typically make most of their money off authors, not book sales.

Again, I felt distraught. I had not known enough to protect my client from this disaster. Suddenly, the books that had been the light of her life for more than a year were becoming sources of great anxiety. Bea sounded deflated, crushed. We talked about suing their company and fought for months to get the rights to her books back. Ultimately, though, Bea was not in favor of litigation, and settled with the company to get the rights to her books back.

It was so painful to watch Bea go through this without being able to do much to improve the situation, but it inspired me to say to myself, "I can do it better." I didn't have the distribution, but I could do what this publisher had promised: I could put the book together, get it online, and make copies available for purchase. I could do it at a fraction of the price they had charged Bea up front, and take only a fraction of the percentage this publisher was taking of the sales. Thus, the idea—the *conviction*—for Writers of the Round Table Press was born.

Of course, I knew that our company didn't have the financial means or the distribution capability to act as any kind of commercial publisher. Instead, we would empower our authors through creating a self-publishing model that was more transparent than others out there. It would also be backed with the expertise we had created in design, marketing, and public relations—if the authors wanted those services. In exchange for clients taking the financial risk, we would take a much lower percentage of ownership and be a professional, communicative, and creative support mechanism.

Bea took us up on our offer and we published both of her books. People were emotionally responding to *Edge!*, but *Millennial Leaders* was more topical. Business leaders found it exciting to have conversations about young people's leadership. Soon, Bea got hooked into the news cycle with radio and television interviews, and the book received excellent reviews. Even to this day, she spends more time on *Millennial Leaders* than *Edge!*, which, out of necessity, was placed on the backburner. I am still hopeful that *Edge!* will find its audience (to that end, we're releasing a comic book version of *Edge!* in 2012!).

Bea and I went to battle together, and I genuinely like and respect her. But even now, I feel horrible that I couldn't prevent her from getting wounded by the industry, that I couldn't keep *Edge!*, which was so beautiful, from being sullied. And once something is sullied, it's hard—almost impossible—to undo the damage. The negative feelings become scar tissue, thick and tough, and how do you move past that to pick up momentum again? Often, it's easier to move on to something else with the lessons you've learned.

It's been a long time since I've talked about this story. It's almost as though the pain was so great that I forgot it, because we forged on. Bea and I still communicate, and I'm thankful that the experience didn't end with animosity toward each other. In situations like this, many people deconstruct the relationship to find reasons why it didn't work, why the goals weren't met, or why the process was ruined. Thankfully, Bea and I never did that.

This is why I feel that my company must be extra protective of every step of our clients' journeys—because at any point, those journeys can become tarnished. And because creation is so damn personal, when it gets tarnished, it feels like it will never be bright again. I'm proud of the fact that we created Writers of the Round Table Press for our clients because of what happened with Bea. But I'm forever saddened that she had to be the one to go through such heartbreak. She did not deserve it.

#J^UMP 10

BEING THE DEVIL IN MY OWN DEAL

ONCE I navigated my first two book projects with Writers of the Round Table, I started becoming confident about my ability to help people with their written stories. The economy was still strong, and people had liquid income, so for a while, we were signing one or two big clients a month. At the same time, one of the writers I had been working with on the business side of the company, was doing well for us and I enjoyed working with her and groomed her to take on more responsibility for the part of the business I no longer wanted to grow. Then we brought in another writer to work more closely with our creative clients.

The company ballooned faster than it should have because we had a lot of immediate revenue coming in from authors who had signed up for book projects. Through it all,

#JUMP

I was pushing and pulling and figuring out how to balance everything, and one day I woke up and thought, *Holy shit! I'm a businessman. How did this happen?* I had employees, and we were driving a couple hundred thousand dollars a year in revenue. Over the course of three years, we pulled in over a million dollars—which may sound small, but I'm still astonished that we accomplished it based on my *idea*. It took willingness to dive into completely unexplored territory, combined with the expertise I'd assembled in team-building and storytelling and leadership. It was a marriage of the two sides of the mind—art and business—and the more I worked with clients, the more I recognized that I loved helping people who were balanced more heavily on one side than the other. In a way, we were producing people's dreams, and that felt right.

But the business was growing so quickly, the excitement so potent, that I made the mistake of getting addicted to selling, of confusing a sale with my own worth.

In 2007, a couple of business owners came to me wanting to write a book. They were affluent and worked in an industry in which, without incredible attention to detail, people would die. They had recently read another of our business books and were floored by the concept. They were so excited that they wanted to write a similarly styled book about their industry, in which they'd worked extensively. And they had a specific request: they wanted to work with the writer of that other book—*but* they wanted their book ghostwritten. Nobody but my clients would receive any credit for the work—not the writer, not my company, not myself.

Before a contract was even prepared, a small voice within me spoke up. If I took on this project, the voice argued, I was going to have two bosses, rather than one. There would be so much going on outside my control. When I work with an individual—as I always had before—everything about the project is discussed with me. What was I going to do, insert myself at their conference table or between them at lunch so that I didn't miss any serious discussions?

The reality was that the majority of work and epiphany would probably occur without me or my team. And without us, there would be no guide to the process; just double the emotions and the complications they could bring. In the best-case scenario, my little voice continued, this project would be exponentially more difficult than ones I'd worked on in the past. At worst, it wouldn't work at all.

Many of the details of this opportunity felt wrong, but I convinced myself that I was Superman and that I could make it work. That tiny, intuitive voice in my head was silenced by my ego, which was chasing the feeling of worthiness that working with these kinds of high-level professionals carried. For so long, I had chased credibility, the validation that comes from working with more prestigious clients. And I thought that these people would provide that, even though the book would be ghostwritten and I wouldn't be able to tell anyone of my role in the project. A normal human being would recognize the disconnect, but I was arrogant enough to believe that the process I brought to the table was so powerful that these people would *want* to share credit—would *want* to be transparent.

My intense desire to close the deal, completely overrode the small voice in me, and I signed the paperwork.

Right away, they made their expectations clear by how closely they reviewed each page of writing. I, too, have high expectations, but I had never come across people who measured every word—in a sixty-thousand word manuscript—what felt like a thousand times. That level of specificity was foreign to me.

As I'd feared in the beginning, the demands from these business owners were more intense than I'd ever experienced with an individual client. The emotions coming from them were also more intense. In this situation, working with two clients was not twice as hard as working with one; it felt four times as challenging because the emotions were multiplied. When the clients felt things, they felt them as a team. In order to resist being pulled into drama that was not going to benefit the book, my focus had to be as intense as their feelings. For the benefit of the book, I tried hard not to play into their fears.

My company's book-writing process for fiction and non-fiction narrative begins with character development. We take clients through the creation stage of discovering who the characters are at their core. We build the people with whom the reader will travel, exploring these characters' backgrounds, hopes, flaws, and frailties. Even though this was a non-fiction manuscript, it would follow the fictional narrative format, which these clients had loved—but they didn't understand or value the character development process. They were completely uninspired and kept saying to me, "We don't know why we're wasting time with this." All I could do was ask for their trust. To their credit, they gave it to me, and though it was arduous, some value was created through that portion of the process, though it was little.

Then we started diving into the chapters of the book. Though the same woman who had written the book they'd so admired was writing their book, the clients hated what she was doing. They hated everything about it: the tone, the details, the dialogue, the style. I was constantly on the phone with them, trying to find solutions. We took a few steps forward and finally felt on track, only to have the writer deliver something that sent them into a tailspin, feeling as though she just didn't get it. After nine months of trying to push through with this writer, encountering resistance from the clients throughout, we had to concede that it just wasn't working. At that point, we made the difficult decision to start over ... without the writer.

So there we were, nine months and immeasurable effort into the project, and we felt like we had gone nowhere. The clients were frustrated by the process, and I was frustrated that my approach wasn't working with them; they were not comfortable with the creative process and how stories organically develop through our approach. Everything just looked permanently and irreversibly like crap to them, and they were reacting accordingly. Yet, we had a lot of integrity with one another and we all worked hard to remain positive. That might be difficult to imagine, considering the process described thus far, but I have to give us all credit for being respectful with one another throughout the challenges. In fact, I think we actually came to care about one another. I know I cared about them, wanted to do well by them, and wanted to deliver what they were looking for. And they knew that if they left this relationship feeling badly about their book, that attitude would be detrimental to its future. From experience, I also knew that this was true.

Needing to find a new path, we changed our arrangement so that I became the story guide and editor, and one of the business owners did the majority of the writing. They needed a lot of guidance, and the writer of the two complained about it frequently, making not-so-subtle innuendos about his dissatisfaction at having to "write" the book he had paid

#JUMP

so much for my team to create. Understandable!

Before he wrote each chapter, we talked for a couple hours about what the goal of each was. Then he would deliver a first draft to me, and I would reshape it from an editorial perspective; after that, we would repeat the process anywhere from five to (literally) thirty times. Then we'd move on to the next chapter. And the lessons kept coming.

Each chapter of this book was followed by a summary, which explored the lessons learned by the characters and showed readers how to apply those lessons to their own lives. For those portions of the book, the clients were adamant that I hire an additional writer. Working with this type of book in the past, I had always made sure that these sections highlighted the real voice of the client, so I felt it was imperative that the sections sounded and felt like my clients. The clients, however, wanted a specific and professional tone and felt they could not do that themselves or with me. So I conceded—despite the fact that, at this point, the book had already cost me as much to produce as they had paid for it.

At a conference I'd recently spoken at, I had met a writer I liked. I made the introductions, and the clients loved him. The future looked promising. I felt I could trust this writer, and, as tensions were building between the clients and I, working with him allowed me the opportunity to step away from the book for a while.

Slowly, the clients introduced the concept of precision to this writer. He and I had numerous conversations where I needed to talk him off the ledge so to speak so he could vent and then get back to work in a professional manner. I couldn't fault him; after all, I understood the challenges of working with them. However, I didn't appreciate that the writer started becoming careless. He incorrectly cited a number of references he had used and refused to admit any wrongdoing on his part. Naturally, this caused my clients to question everything he had written. I had to pay for some pricey plagiarism detection software to ensure that the material was safe. For the most part, we appeared fine, but the clients decided to rewrite most of his work anyway as a safeguard.

My little voice and I were now having full-on conversations. I was way past the point of trying to fool myself about the true cost of taking on this project. I lay in bed at two or three in the morning, eyes wide open, head spinning in a million directions. I was drowning in the feelings of being undervalued, of not being appreciated, and of having to pay for my clients' extreme desire for perfection. I was so angry at the world for not taking care of me. Here I was, making difficult choices that were costing my company a lot of money because it was the right thing to do, and the world was not making it any easier; in fact, the world was making the process even tougher.

I was also angry with myself. After all, *I*, and no one else, had put myself in this position. Yes, I had made my deal with the devil, but that devil was *me!* It was *my* deal. *I* had gone after the clients, named the price, and structured the agreement. I had no one to blame but myself. At times, it felt as though the bitterness was oozing out of me. I had anxious stomachaches and sleepless nights. It got to where I was creating conversations with the clients in my head— telling them something, imagining their responses, getting angry about their foreseen reactions, and then acting out my anger in real life. I had to be on guard against creating self-fulfilling prophecies so that I could get on the phone with them and be kind and productive.

#JUMP

As of June 2008, I was no longer getting paid for my work on the project, and all the way through April 2010, I was still working on final edits and hiring outside help to review the client's continual questions and needs for further perfection. Yes, this contract with a predetermined fee turned out to be a financial disaster. I remember times when I would call up another member of our team and furiously pace around because I was so upset at the conflict between my integrity—which said, *This is your word, you said you were going to deliver this, and you're going to do whatever it takes*—and the reality that the company was losing a large amount of money for my choice.

At the end of the day, I still get worked up about this project, because it taught me painful lessons for years and continues to do so. To my benefit, that pain has taught me so much about my business and about my choices. I have to give these clients a lot of credit because they didn't know any better; they had never been a part of this industry before and they trusted me to guide them. I simply didn't know what was going to be required by their extreme personalities.

In late 2009, their book was placed with a major literary agency. That victory felt deliciously bittersweet. On the one hand, to have created an exceptional product together after so much turmoil was thrilling. On the other, it was full of sorrow. After four years of contributing to their book, I would receive zero credit for assisting. My name would not even appear in the acknowledgments; in fact, another editor, who had put in about fifty hours, would receive credit for my thousand hours or more of contribution. My only benefit was the education. And painful as it is to say, it was a valuable education. At this point, I feel as though I've earned my doctorate several times over.

As a result of this experience, I no longer offer myself or my employees as a ghostwriter because I recognize how much we personally put into such projects. We also no longer offer flat fees for our book packaging process so that no matter how much attention to detail a client requests, we can deliver happily (huge lesson!).

I am proud of myself for having lived my high priced consequence out in the best way possible. I kept my word, and regardless of how tedious the journey (for them too I'm positive!), we treated one another with integrity and respect—two things that are priceless in business.

Unfortunately, after six months, the clients separated from their agent, who had not been successful trying to sell their book to a major publisher. Once again, I watched my clients be disappointed by a difficult publishing industry. And of course, that means they wanted to vanity publish … and that required a whole extra round of edits and formatting, which I did for free. I'm a glutton for punishment, but a man of my word.

#J^UMP 11

GETTING THE SALE VS. DOING THE WORK

IN the end, people pay me for a product. But I actually feel that I earn my money through process. I've worked hard and learned through my many jumps to build a creative process that is flexible, dynamic, exciting, frightening, and illuminating for my clients. It's through this means that they find their true stories, and for me, it's a privilege to be a part of their journey of self-discovery.

There was a period of time when I was learning how to be a salesperson for the company. A prospective client was on the line, and it was a good-sized job. I had not signed on a new book-writing client in a while, and I was hungry both to drive revenue and to add another book to our pipeline for potential publishing. I had not yet done enough investigation into the previous book debacle with the two business owners to analyze where I made a mess of things, so this time, I was more excited to *sell* than to actually do the job. As a business owner, you wear many hats, and I was flexing my sales muscle. This client was almost ready to sign, but as part of the condition of the sale, he stipulated that I be the one to write his book.

"Look," I said, "I'm not a great writer. And I'm busy. The process will be much more effective if you let me hire a writer while I guide the process." He wouldn't agree, and I caved quickly, desiring to move from the sales process into whatever was next.

Over the next year, I did enough to fulfill my obligation, but I didn't care about the client's story in the way that I needed to. I was desperately trying to keep the company afloat amidst tough economic times, and I was addicted to learning how to do that. Though I felt an undercurrent of guilt, I was so busy trying to pay the bills every month that I continued avoiding my obligation to this client.

This meant that, unlike my work in the past, I was not creating a process for this client by which *he* was being pushed to find his truth. Instead, we would speak on the phone, he would "court report" what had happened in his life, and I would record and take notes. He experienced no epiphanies because I was not forcing him to dive deeper. He was no different one year later than when we had started, and I felt that I hadn't earned my money. Sure, I had written a first full draft, but it was flat and unimpressive—a mere factual account of his life with no emotion behind it. In agreeing to the condition of his contract, I let myself be talked into doing something that would not benefit him in the end.

There's real sadness to a situation like this. My client's story was an important one that wasn't being told importantly;

it wasn't doing what a story can do. This was his life journey, and, from a writing perspective, not doing justice to someone's life journey is devastating. I couldn't help but feel that, when he died someday, his story would die with him if I didn't create a legacy for him. I had helped him put his life into words but in a way that was more like a journal than an experience that invited readers to empathize with what he had been through. And while I felt frustration for him and anger at myself, I also understood how this had happened and talked myself into believing that it was not entirely my own responsibility. There are failed leaps in business, as I'd experienced many times already. Not everything can be a great success story. I asked myself if this was just one of those times.

And then one day I was sitting across from my therapist and the anxiety of failing this client hit me over the head. I could not live with myself if I did not do this man justice. That afternoon, I called him and recommended that he and I take a trip. "For five days," I said, "we'll seclude ourselves. I'll focus completely on you and this story, and we'll *force* something great to happen with the book."

My client agreed.

To make sure we got as much work done as possible, we decided to go grocery shopping before settling in at the cottage I'd rented. We'd cook all our meals there and create an environment in which we could be both creative and productive. In a way, I was seeking to recreate the experience I'd had in the cabin in Mammoth with the other actors in Elevation 9000. The difference in this case was that this client and I weren't familiar with each other. We'd only shared one meal together, and that was in a restaurant when we'd first met.

#J^UMP

Grocery shopping is an entirely difference experience when the person whose cart you're sharing is a stranger. You get to know each other in an oddly intimate way: What kind of food does the other person buy? What brands? How do they feed themselves? I knew that my client had grown up on a farm, but I *really* knew it by the things he was buying—lots of onions and beans. No meat but twelve cans of sardines. Four boxes of Nutrigrain granola bars (for five days). Here I was buying sandwich meat and cheese, chicken breasts, and frozen broccoli. We were from two different worlds, and I was nervous but excited for what was to come.

The grocery store experience set the stage for the rest of the trip. We were on the east coast, and it was gorgeous with colors. He drove me by some of the places I'd heard about in the book we were writing. I saw his old high school and the corner where he'd gotten into a nasty fight that nearly killed another boy and could have changed the course of my client's life forever. I saw the farm where he had lived by himself when he was fourteen years old. I saw the pond that he'd built.

But while we were driving, he was already beginning to tell me stories I had heard before. I just kept thinking, *Oh God, oh God*, as I feared we might simply regurgitate what we'd already done over the last year. There was a cavernous gap between some of the things he found interesting and the things I found interesting, from a storyteller's perspective—something that comes up with most clients. Every person I have worked with has trouble being objective about his or her own life; that's natural. But I had always been able to handle it in small doses of sixty to ninety minutes. Being stuck together for five days straight would require more of me.

We eventually made it to the cottage and started to work—quickly. I set up my workstation in the dining area and dove in. I would lead my client in fleshing out stories he had previously told me, and then I would jump into each chapter until I was happy with it and felt it captured an essence of him. He would read through it, we would discuss his impressions, and I would revise before moving on. We were making some dynamite progress and breezed through the first half of the book. I was seeing him smile as he watched it coming together, and I felt great that we had made the decision to do this. The process was working.

For five days, he continued to tell me stories while I recorded everything we were saying. Each time I thought I saw an important nugget for the book, I'd email Erin, now our Directoress of Happiness, to get that conversation transcribed. Bless her heart, she'd turn those around lightning-fast, and then, sitting at the high kitchen table whose chairs made the backs of my legs sore, I'd take those nuggets and shape them, pushing myself to get the writing done right then rather than wait until morning. My client prepared meals for us while I wrote, so as I was hearing his stories, I was also tasting his cooking. I was seeing how a guy who grew up alone from the age of fourteen puts food together. It was like nothing I'd ever eaten, and it was delicious. He knew how to cook beans and onions so that they wouldn't give a person gas!

"I loved beans growing up," he explained, "and I had to figure out a way to cook them so that I could digest them, go to work, and use them as fuel."

That was a wonderfully fascinating part of this trip. When you're together in such a close environment, the story is not entirely told through voice. When you see a person shuffle out of their bedroom at six a.m. and say good morning, you get to know who they are. And when it's late into the night and they can't sleep, you understand them in a different way. Somehow, all of that gets infused into the work.

But all that said, it was *hard!* I deliberately set up my business so that I do things in short bursts—ten or fifteen minutes at a time, an hour-long phone call, etc. But here, I had to listen for hours. Sometimes we'd forget to eat, and all the while, I'd be sifting through material, trimming ninety percent of what he said to get to the real story. The exercise of figuring out what was going to be in the book and what was extraneous, of taking care of myself by letting him know when we were too far off path, was difficult, even harmful to my creative process. It was frustrating to be writing a passage we'd just talked about only to have him suddenly dive into a new thought or epiphany. I found myself getting angry, because I couldn't listen to him *and* do the task at hand.

Halfway through our five days together I finally figured out how to deal with that anger: I discovered that to nurture him as a client, the way I wanted to, I had to say, "I need ten minutes to write." He'd busy himself with other things, and I'd write without interruption to keep myself from crashing. Because I wanted to do good work for him, to do his story justice, it was difficult for me to take care of myself that way. Yet, the results echoed those of enforcing professional boundaries with Angelica Harris: only through taking care of myself could I fully take care of this client.

Still, the environment was challenging. We were working with the pressured knowledge that we only had five days. I knew we needed to be in great shape by the end of our time together in order to get the project back on track. We had no time to waste. With that in mind, I learned to direct the show.

At one point, he was telling a story, and I interrupted to say, "Your reader's asleep."

He looked at me. "What?"

"Your reader's asleep," I repeated.

"Oh," he said. "Okay!" He got it and we moved on.

During the process, I realized that he was a little kid telling a story. He didn't know what was important and what wasn't. He was just fleshing it out and waiting to be prompted. He was teaching me about directing the show as much as I was teaching him how to build his story.

At the end of the second day, we were interrupted by a horrendous rainstorm—the worst the east coast had seen in five years. We actually had to move his car at one point so it wouldn't float away. We took it to the farm, which was expansive, but because nothing was being grown, the field looked like bunches of balled up dirt and grass. There was a run-down farmhouse and behind it, on a big hill, a large beautiful house that he had built and then ended up selling as an equestrian center. It was a weird atmosphere of old and new, a collision of past and present.

We pulled up next to a huge super-duty truck with massive wheels and left the car there. We drove the truck back to the cottage, but by that time, rain was a foot and a half up the house (which, fortunately, was built on stilts). We ended up getting completely rained in; we had to wrap trash bags around our legs just to get to the car. In a sense, we were prisoners, both to the cottage and our project.

The project itself was unique to me because it became like a murder mystery I had to solve. The story is a search for the meaning of color, the meaning of personal and racial identity, but much of it is steeped in my client's search for his birth mother—a hunt that spanned twenty years and a *lot* of information. He had three huge binders that were each about nine inches thick, packed with the evidence of a two-decade quest. I had to sift through this information in order to take the reader through experiencing the first clue, the second one, the third, and so on. God bless him for saving everything and having it damn well organized. Still, it was daunting to figure out what was relevant, what would be included in the book—and in what order—so that readers would feel that they were solving the riddle just as he had done years before and I was doing now.

On the last night at the cottage, we decided that we'd begin his book with a letter to his mother, written the night before he was to meet her for the first time. The letter would hold everything he wanted to say, everything he didn't want to forget to ask when he met her. It seemed like the final, perfect piece to the puzzle that putting this book together had become.

My five days at the cottage with my client were a wild experience. More than anything, it was permission to let everything else go. I had asked my staff not to e-mail me unless it was urgent and not to copy me on e-mails that I could go without seeing. I talked to my wife for, at most, ten minutes a day. And though I was finally able to tame my own attention deficit disorder (which I didn't know I had until then!), I also had to adapt to my client's style of working. He sleeps little and works hard, up to eighteen or nineteen hours at a time. I would have set it up to where we worked for eight or ten hours a day, set aside time for meals, and then retreated to our own spaces for the night and got together again in the morning. I would have thought that I'd be a train wreck doing it his way. But while it was challenging, there was also something cathartic about doing something so foreign to me, about proving to myself that I *could* do it. It was confidence building, and it goes back to what I always say: "If you don't change through the process of writing your book, don't expect anyone to be changed through the process of reading it." I realized that it's not only the client who must change, but the whole story team, and I was being forced to do my share.

When my client dropped me off at the airport at the end of the trip, we shared a beautifully awkward moment where I shook his hand and said, "This was a great experience, and I'm excited about what we've created." He had this look on his face and a smile that was like a five-year-old kid's, and he said, "Yeah, this is good. This is real good." He put out his hand to give me a fist bump, and I thought that he wanted to give me a hug. Maybe to thank me because I had given him a five-day retreat to just be with his mother, to sit without interruption in that world of the search he'd taken. And I wanted to give *him* a hug because his participation in this trip had given me the opportunity to regain my integrity around this project. I had done right by his story, and that freed me.

We didn't give each other that hug. We did the fist bump and nodded, and then I left. Afterward, I couldn't help getting emotional. The story of the search for his mother and his own identity was, and is, so powerful. In his search, he faced discrimination from both sides of the spectrum: He was a mixed child, and while whites didn't want to claim him; neither did blacks. Germany, where his mother was from, didn't want him; did America? His adoptive parents didn't care for him. He was tossed away by society. And when he finally found his mother, he was met with more tragedy. Considering the difficult and lonely road he had traveled as an adolescent, it's incredible that he didn't grow into a homeless, bitter adult. Instead, he went on to partner his farming skills with science, which he would use in more than a dozen third world countries, setting up equipment that would allow millions of cancer patients to be treated inexpensively with radiation. His story exemplifies human triumph—going from a perceived idiot, which people thought he was as a child, to an education addict to a conduit of healing. It was awe-inspiring and emotionally overwhelming to be part of.

I thought about all this at the airport, about how I had gotten to know this man's story from more than just his words. Everything, from the car he picked me up in to the way he cooked beans to the twelve cans of sardines to the eighteen-hour workdays, told me something about his life. His is a beautiful story that I was honored to tell, and after we said goodbye, I noticed myself standing tall and looking around at people as they passed me in the airport. I didn't see the other travelers as obstacles between the security check-in gate and the terminal, as I often do; I saw them as people with stories that were worth telling and worth hearing.

#J^UMP 12

FROM THE BARRIO TO THE BOARD ROOM AND THE TRANSFORMATIONAL POWER OF STORY

WHEN I started working with Robert Renteria in 2006, Writers of the Round Table was still in its infancy. Robert's assistant had posted a description of his project, a memoir, on the website where I had experienced so much success bidding on projects. He needed someone to help him write the story of his life, in hopes that it would inspire and motivate others to work hard to actualize their dreams. Despite not having worked on any other book than Angelica's by that time, I believed that I could help him.

I remember walking up to Robert's office building and buzzing in at the front door the first time we met. He came

#JUMP

down and held the door open for me, smiled and welcomed me inside. It was that small, simple act of kindness that immediately sold me on Robert, and I was hungry to work with him. I sat across from him in his conference room, listened to some of the details of his life, and knew he had a story that could inspire powerful change. Though I'm not sure he noticed, I got emotional while listening to him. Something about his story hit a deep nerve with me. I was confident that I could paint a written picture of his life and that my filmmaker's point of view could be directed at a book. Robert agreed.

We spent a number of weeks on our contract to ensure that we were in agreement on how our relationship would be defined. Coming from the corporate world, Robert brought in an attorney who was aggressive and worked to push the agreement in Robert's favor. I was looking for a win-win—a contract that equally favored both of us. At one point, I had to call Robert and tell him that if working with him on the book was going to be as difficult as navigating this contract, we were going to have a problem. We had to be a team, I stipulated. He agreed, pulled back his attorney, and he and I hashed out the specifics of the deal so that we could dive into his stories.

To start, Robert told me that his entertainment as a toddler was counting the fat, hairy cockroaches that scuttled across the walls of his tiny East L.A. home. His family was so poor and had so few possessions that he slept in a dresser drawer at night. His mother worked hard and instilled in him from a young age that he could do anything with *ganas* (guts) and *orgullo* (pride). Robert's father, however, abandoned the family in search of heroin and alcohol when Robert was only three, leaving Robert's mother to work two and three jobs to support the family and make sure they did not become part of the system.

Robert would need both *ganas* and *orgullo* to survive the world in which he grew up. Despite his mother's honest, positive influence, he got sucked into a tough street crowd at a young age. He ran with gangs, did drugs and sold them, was stabbed and shot at, and could have lost his life and future at any given moment—just as his father eventually did. When Robert was seventeen, his father died, and Robert went to Skid Row to collect the few sad items remaining of a man he'd never known.

One day, Robert's grandfather made a bet with him: "If you left here and came back to this place ten years from now, you'd see that all of your so-called friends were either dead or in jail." It took three years, but Robert finally accepted that challenge, and it was the beginning of a new life for him—a life in which he found himself addicted to work and its effect on his life. A true example of beating the odds, Robert went back to school for his GED, served our country as a non-commissioned officer in the U.S. Army for more than seven years as an elite soldier, and wound up climbing the corporate ladder until he was the most successful commercial coin laundry professional the industry had ever seen. Then he stepped off that ladder, which he found to be quite broken, to return to what he loved: his customers. That was when he took the shot and opened his own business and stunned those who didn't believe Robert could be as successful as he had dreamed.

Robert and I spent a year and a half writing his book *From the Barrio to the Board Room*. I would ask questions, often via email, and he would respond by telling me his stories. I would probe one area and then the next, and Robert was the near perfect client, always willing to move in any direction I felt we needed to explore. I pushed him to reveal some of the more humiliating aspects of his past, and as he learned to trust the process—and me—his book began to take real shape. When we were done, he felt a palpable excitement about the book's potential. So did I.

We repeatedly tested the book on focus groups, and the response was tremendous right off the bat: though readers had differing opinions about certain sections, more than eighty percent were hooked from the beginning. That was how I knew we had a winner. My creative director at the time, Nathan Brown, designed the brilliant cover, and, as Writers of the Round Table Press had not yet been created, we worked with a printing consultant to self-publish two thousand copies that we could use in an initial push.

That's when the magic began. With only a few hundred books out on the street, Robert was getting phone calls and e-mails from readers, and being stopped in the street by strangers. The book was having a profound impact on both children and adults: kids were leaving gangs; they were going back to school; and they were getting better grades, staying away from drugs, and disassociating with gangs. Adults were starting their own businesses, moving their families out of Section 8 housing, and spending more time with their kids.

How could Robert deny that he had created something that was working? And, upon seeing its effect, how could we *not* step up and offer this new tool to those who were battling the issues his book addressed? Still, Robert didn't quite believe it was possible, so we continued to test it. We tested it with kids. We tested it with political figures. We tested it with teachers and parents. The effect was undeniable.

It's amazing how long it takes someone to believe that he or she can impact a large number of people—and then buy into it in thought and in action. Robert spent three and a half of the five plus years we've worked together in disbelief. But, just as I did with Bea Fields and *Edge!*, I bought into the power of Robert's story right from the beginning. And because I had been putting out creative work for years and had learned how to gauge people's truthful reactions, I knew this book had power. I was a quick barometer, knew where this could go, and led the charge beside Robert.

My goal was to hit Chicago, L.A., and New York, but Robert first wanted to make a change in his hometown of nearly twenty-one years, so we targeted Aurora, Illinois, a city of 100,000 people. For a year and a half, we worked aggressively to get the book into as many hands as we could. We sold books, gifted books, and found donors for books who would buy them in bulk. We collected feedback from kids, schools, teachers, and parents ... and then repeated, repeated, repeated.

The feedback became addictive. It was a rush of excitement to hear that we were changing lives. Robert and I both have addictive personalities, and the sheer amount and type of comments from readers sent us diving wholeheartedly into getting Robert's book and message into even more hands.

And what results! We had kids stealing the books from classrooms. We had parents introducing us to teachers and principals. We got an e-mail from a mother who was giving her gangbanger son a copy of the book—but he couldn't carry it in public or talk about Robert because, in the gang, it was a violation! Gangs were paying Robert a strange kind of respect by recognizing him as a threat. For me, the idea of sneaking books to kids because they couldn't be seen with

#J^UMP

those titles in public opened my eyes to a world I had only heard about in the news.

After that year and a half of concentrating our efforts on a relatively small scale, we expanded to Chicago. Robert met Mayor Richard Daley. The Secretary of State of Illinois, Jesse White, endorsed the book by inviting Robert to keynote the state's Hispanic Heritage Reception and awarding him as an author. Our 2nd Edition of the book (October 2011) has a foreword written by Illinois State Senator Iris Martinez. The book is also used in youth prisons and Robert recently spoke to 300 inmates at the Cook County Jail in Chicago. We've presented to Principals from around the country and Robert spoke to 700 students and faculty at the Chicago School of Professional Psychology. We're traveling in circles of real decision-makers, and these people are telling us the same thing: "We're spending millions of dollars trying to tackle the gang and drug problem in traditional ways that are only effective on paper, and here you guys come in the back door with something unconventional that actually works—something we never could have created." But we reached these people because of the pattern of repetition we created, of garnering feedback that we could share with others to inspire their buy-in.

I have to admit that even I have been surprised at how much goes into making space in people's minds for this kind of work. You have to get into their psyches, which is extremely difficult in this Internet age where everyone is bombarded with information from a million directions, as well as into their unique pressures and expectations, dreams and desires.

I think what authors have a hard time comprehending is that you can be a storyteller, but if you want to be a world-changer, there is a divide that has to be crossed. You must be desperate enough (or insane enough) to make an impact that you are willing to invest equal amounts of time, emotion, and money to do so. The truth is that it's brutal. It *has* to be: there are more than six billion great ideas in the world (everybody has at least one), and yours has to be far more than a great idea to inspire real change. *You* have to be far more than great in your desire. When the world pushes, do you have enough in you to push back hard, over and over again? Do you have what it takes to create a brand that takes people out of their already cluttered lives and inspires them to look at your story and then at themselves? That's the divide. These are the questions I have to ask my clients. And, I suppose, myself.

I've created a number of books for people who hoped that, after the writing, their work was done. It's the way I thought years ago—that if I was a talented enough actor or filmmaker, the rest would somehow take care of itself. But I've learned through my continual willingness to jump that an artist of any kind must approach their business from four different angles: product development, networking, marketing, and public relations. You cannot rely solely on being creative. You have to put your business hat on, too. And you have to be open to unexpected opportunities.

Our most unexpected opportunity with *Barrio* came in 2009, when teachers began approaching us with the desire to use the book formally. We had worked closely with teachers all along, but it never occurred to us that the book—the journey—would move so far in this direction. Yet I recognized that the teachers were right: just as the book was working as a non-traditional way to tackle the gang and drug problem, it could be a unique teaching tool in classrooms. We worked to develop a curriculum, a two-week course around the book, that would later be called "From the Barrio to the Classroom" (my wife titled this one!). The school curriculum was a new way to help people hear and use Robert's story and to date more than 10,000 students have participated.

When I first started pushing the curriculum, I don't think Robert understood why. But I wanted to take students on the journey Robert had been on—turning his previously troubled life into one that was meaningful. Robert is feeling the joy of life now, absorbing every ounce of it in a way that few people do, and the curriculum was designed as a way for kids to use Robert's story as a model for telling their own.

Every day, students are pelted with questions seeking informative answers. What is the answer to this math problem? Who is the author of that book? What is the date of that historical event? They are not often asked to engage personally with one another. But with this course, teachers lead their students through two weeks of exercises that help them reveal parts of themselves that they don't expose in their everyday environment.

The idea is that, when people can articulate their stories, they can be seen in three dimensions instead of one. So when the kids answer these questions and tell their own stories, they feel as if they're part of something. When you feel visible in the world, you're more confident. And when you're more confident, you make better choices. The process is working and storytelling is the impetus.

When we began developing this curriculum, I never told anybody the storytelling angle. Nowhere is it written that the curriculum is based on the notion that storytelling can help kids get to know one another, to pull away from judgment and cliques and nastiness. I sensed that, if I laid it out that way, people wouldn't buy into it. But it's happening.

Once these kids finally see the "parts" of others that make them three-dimensional—that make them human—the kids change. Their worlds change.

That's what happened to Robert when he shared his story. He became visible to the world. People feel as though they know him because of how much he revealed in his book, and they adore him (or can't stand him) because he's three-dimensional to them.

In helping Robert tell his story, I stumbled onto a hidden agenda of my own. Ultimately, I wish every school would help its students articulate their own stories, whether through Robert's curriculum or another one, because, if these kids understood who they were, they wouldn't be so impressionable to negative opportunities. They wouldn't need a gang to define who they are.

Imagine a young kid being approached to sell drugs for an older child. If the kid knows who he or she is and what his or her values are, they'll be more likely to say no. Imagine a junior in high school who is interviewing at colleges. Because she knows how to articulate herself, admissions committees can see her potential. When we know how to voice our own stories, we know ourselves.

The same year we created the teaching curriculum, Robert and I released a Spanish version of *Barrio*, and then started the From the Barrio Foundation. Earlier in 2011, we released a comic book version called *Mi Barrio* (foreword by Linda Chapa LaVia, Illinois House of Representatives) that is being used in both languages to reach more of those who need this message of hope. At the time of writing this book, Robert is about to receive a humanitarian award in Chicago. The momentum is only picking up, and I'm realizing how many ways there are to reach people through story.

#J^UMP

Finally, after so many lessons, I've learned how to navigate the creative process and come out on the other side, still in a trusting relationship with my creative partner—in this case, Robert. I've finally been able to market our work the way it deserves. I think that's the beautiful power of story: you have no idea what's going to happen with it, but if you're open to it and put it out into the world, the people who *need* it will find it. And sometimes, the person who needs it most is the one you least expect: yourself.

For more information on From the Barrio and author Robert Renteria, please visit www.fromthebarrio.com.

AFTERWORD

AT Round Table Companies, we focus on sharing big stories in business and life, and in filtering those stories through the hearts, souls, and unique voices of the authors we work with. I feel blessed to have had such a steep learning curve. Had I been a business major who was forced to learn creativity later in life, I don't think I could have developed a business as wonderful and impacting as RTC. Painful as my lessons in business have been, I discovered that business skills can be learned. Learning creativity at an older age sounds like too large an obstacle to have overcome. But because my DNA was creative at its roots, and my belief in the ability of storytelling to impact the world was so strong, I had a reason to dust myself off as I learned how to better serve our clients and employees, and those lessons have yielded a better business.

Michael Gerber, whom I was fortunate to spend time with at three "In the Dreaming Room" events he hosted, captured it best when he built his new business model around a simple, deeply meaningful concept: that a dream should be at the center of any relevant business. So many business owners open their businesses because they "make sense" rather than their passion being so strong that they have no choice.

As I'm looking back over the contents of this book, at all the times I jumped and fell and thought my spirit had been crushed, I feel thankful for the leaps that didn't pan out as I'd hoped. That willingness to jump and the pain of failure forced me to learn better ways to work, to grow. In the end, the lessons were profound and necessary and have allowed us to support more amazing people, while granting us access to extraordinary industry and media support.

One of my biggest joys is being around a group of people with whom I can build something creative, learning with a family of peers and colleagues who are willing to jump with me. I first found that in L.A., when I initiated the trip to the cabin in Mammoth as an antidote to how alienated I was feeling on commercial and TV sets. Then I repeated that process, that search for a creative family, with each film I did, and now with Writers of the Round Table and Round Table Companies. I've always intuitively understood that, until you nurture relationships, you can't build trust—and without trust that is earned in the trenches, people will not leap into the unknown with you.

Years ago, when I started Writers of the Round Table, if I could have looked into the future and seen what we're doing now, I would have said, "That's f-ing cool!" I recognize that what we've achieved would have been considered by most as impossible. We're literally changing the way non-fiction books are written and published, while also introducing an entirely new market around non-fiction graphic novels, and both have been a tall order that took time and focus. As you've now read, I had to learn how to structure our relationships with our clients, how to attract the ideal client who had both a big message and a big enough budget to engage our team approach, how to cultivate the players in our virtual organization, how to generate the necessary momentum required to get to the end-zone intact, and how to care for our clients on both sides of the equation (creatively and professionally).

With a solid list of partners and a growing team of writers, editors, designers, illustrators, digital strategists, social networking phenoms, and PR pros, the future for Round Table is bright and exciting. Even now, so few people know they have an alternative to hiring a single ghostwriter. So few have any idea what it's like to have the support of an entire team that's on the cutting edge of communication. So few have yet to see that traditional publishing, full of all its gatekeepers, might not be the best choice for their needs. And so I'm off again on my next adventure. As our amazing staff nurtures our clients and their projects, I'm being sent out into the world as an evangelist for our new approach to this industry. Carl Smith, the brilliant founder of web design firm nGen Works, put it best when he described his similar role as the P.T. Barnum of his the company—the barker at the fair out educating the world about what we do. I imagine this will encompass the next couple years of my life and then I'll jump into yet another role.

What I've come to realize over the years is that the goal of jumping is not to reach the ground; it's to learn to stay in flight. There's something both beautiful and terrifying about how hard it is to leap with clients and projects that strive to impact lives on a grand scale, only to search for a horizon that keeps changing, that gets farther away and harder to reach as aspirations grow.

My hope is that you'll be willing to jump again as well. And to recognize your willingness to jump as a step toward reaching the knowledge, lessons, and wisdom you need to align your voice with your work and to make yourself visible in a world that needs your stories. So fall on your face, make a mess of life, and learn something brilliant. If you're jumping, you're learning how to fly, and that's worth celebrating.

ABOUT THE AUTHOR

COREY has been communicating creatively for over 15 years, first as the face and voice behind a dozen Fortune 500 and Fortune 100 brands as a commercial and voiceover actor, then as a film producer and director, as an author and publisher, and now as the founder and President of Round Table Companies, Writers of the Round Table Inc., and Writers of the Round Table Press. Authors published by Corey include Chris Anderson (editor, WIRED Magazine), Tony Hsieh (CEO Zappos), Marshall Goldsmith (prolific executive coach), and new talent such as Robert Renteria, Alesia Shute, and Angelica Harris. Corey is the co-author of numerous books, including *Edge! A Leadership Story* (Finalist 2008 National Best Books Awards) and *From the Barrio to the Board Room* and its companion comic book *Mi Barrio* (Winner, Independent Publisher Book Awards, 2011), which are being used around the country in schools and youth prisons to inspire at-risk youth.

Corey's work has been covered by the *New York Times, Wall Street Journal, USA Today, Forbes, Inc. Magazine, Wired Magazine, Barron's, Publisher's Weekly, School Library Journal,* the *Chicago Sun-Times, Fox News, Bloomberg TV,* and *Investor's Business Daily*. His work has won Addy, Belding, Bronze

#JUMP

Lion, and London International Advertising awards and he has been published in *The Writer Magazine*, *Script* magazine and on *StartUp Nation*.

Corey is a 1996 graduate of Millikin University. He is married to Dr. Dawn Blake, a psychologist, and is the proud father of two precocious pups named Max and Daisy.

The rise of commercially available laptops gives birth to a popular stereotype: **the wanna-be writer.**

Today (with an RTC team).

OTHER TITLES
from

EDGE!
A LEADERSHIP STORY

FOR THOSE WHO LEAD IN BUSINESS
AND THOSE WHO LEAD IN LIFE

BY BEA FIELDS AND COREY BLAKE
WITH EVA SILVA TRAVERS

WITH A FOREWORD BY MICHAEL E. GERBER,
AUTHOR OF THE E-MYTH BOOKS

Becoming A GREAT LEADER

[Lessons from Silicon Valley]

GUSTAVO RABIN Ph.D.

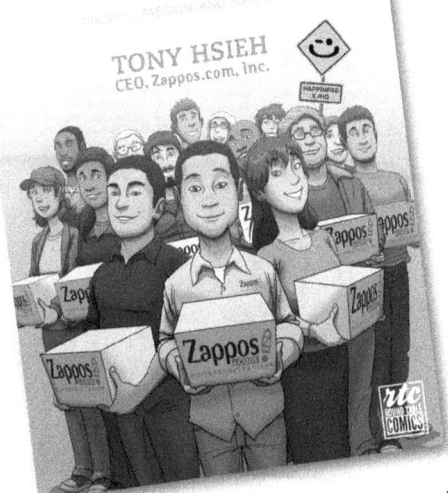

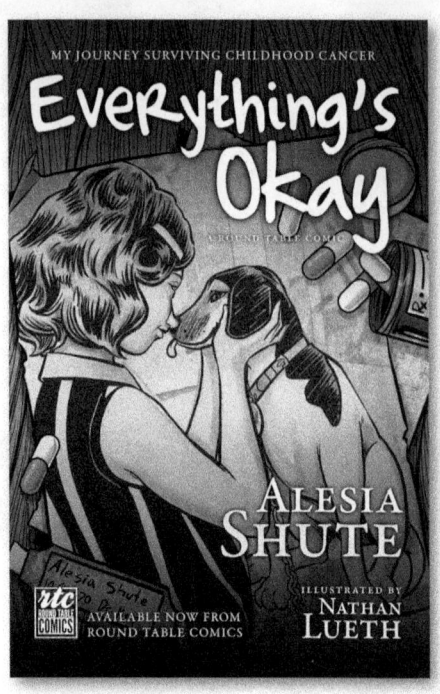

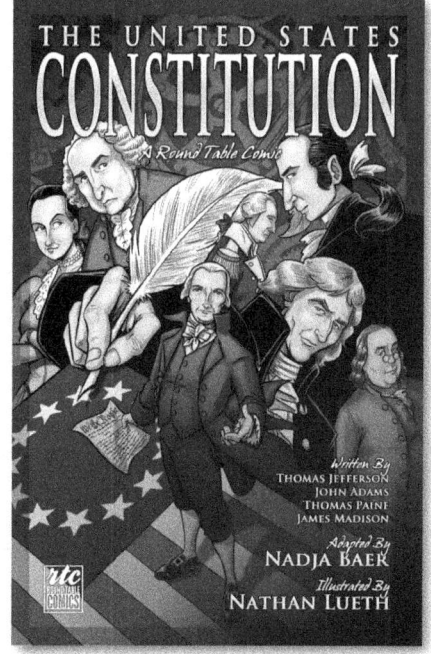

www.ingramcontent.com/pod-product-compliance
Lightning Source LLC
Chambersburg PA
CBHW060838050426
42453CB00008B/735